best ever
pasta sauces

best ever
pasta sauces

the heart of Italian cooking

linda fraser

HERMES HOUSE

This edition is published by Hermes House,

an imprint of Anness Publishing Ltd,
Hermes House, 88–89 Blackfriars Road,
London SE1 8HA;
tel. 020 7401 2077; fax 020 7633 9499

www.hermeshouse.com; www.annesspublishing.com

If you like the images in this book and would like to investigate using them for publishing,
promotions or advertising, please visit our website www.practicalpictures.com for more information.

Publisher: Joanna Lorenz
Cookery Editors: Rosemary Wilkinson, Linda Doeser
Designers: Bill Mason, Siân Keogh
Illustrator: Anna Koska

Recipes: Catherine Atkinson, Carla Capalbo, Maxine Clark, Roz Denny, Christine France, Sarah Gates, Shirley Gill,
Norma MacMillan, Sue Maggs, Elizabeth Martin, Annie Nichols, Jenny Stacy, Liz Trigg, Laura Washburn, Steven
Wheeler
Photographs: Karl Adamson, Edward Allwright, David Armstrong, Steve Baxter, Jo Brewer, James Duncan, Michelle
Garrett, Amanda Heywood, Patrick McLeavey, Michael Michaels
Stylists: Madeleine Brehaut, Jo Brewer, Carla Capalbo, Michelle Garrett, Hilary Guy, Amanda Heywood, Patrick
McLeavey, Blake Minton, Kirsty Rawlings, Elizabeth Wolf-Cohen
Food for Photography: Wendy Lee, Lucy McKelvie, Jane Stevenson, Elizabeth Wolf-Cohen

ETHICAL TRADING POLICY

At Anness Publishing we believe that business should be conducted in an ethical and ecologically sustainable way, with
respect for the environment and a proper regard to the replacement of the natural resources we employ.

As a publisher, we use a lot of wood pulp to make high-quality paper for printing, and that wood commonly comes
from spruce trees. We are therefore currently growing more than 500,000 trees in two Scottish forest plantations near
Aberdeen – Berrymoss (130 hectares/320 acres) and West Touxhill (125 hectares/305 acres). The forests we manage
contain twice the number of trees employed each year in paper-making for our books.

Because of this ongoing ecological investment programme, you, as our customer, can have the pleasure and
reassurance of knowing that a tree is being cultivated on your behalf to naturally replace the materials used to make
the book you are holding.

Our forestry programme is run in accordance with the UK Woodland Assurance Scheme (UKWAS) and will be
certified by the internationally recognized Forest Stewardship Council (FSC). The FSC is a non-government
organization dedicated to promoting responsible management of the world's forests. Certification ensures forests are
managed in an environmentally sustainable and socially responsible basis. For further information about this scheme,
go to www.annesspublishing.com/trees

A CIP catalogue record for this book is available from the British Library

Previously published as part of a larger compendium: *Best-Ever Pasta*

NOTES
For all recipes, quantities are given in both metric and imperial measures and, where appropriate, measures are
given in standard cups and spoons. Follow one set, but not a mixture, because they are not interchangeable.

Standard spoon and cup measurements are level. 1 tsp = 5ml, 1 tbsp = 15ml; 1 cup = 250ml/8fl oz

Australian standard tablespoons are 20ml. Australian readers should use 3 tsp in place of 1 tbsp
for measuring small quantities of gelatine, cornflour, salt etc.

Medium (US large) eggs should be used unless otherwise stated.

CONTENTS

~

Introduction

Virtually anything and everything goes with pasta: meat, poultry, vegetables, fish, seafood, cheese, eggs, cream, herbs. It is one of the world's most versatile and adaptable foods – as well as being nourishing, economic and easy to cook. Sauces for pasta can be as quick and simple or as elaborate and rich as you like.

There are no hard-and-fast rules about what pasta shape to serve with which sauce. However, as a general rule, long, thin, smooth pastas, such as spaghetti, tagliarini and fettuccine, are best suited to lighter and simpler sauces. Short, curly and fluted shapes, such as fusilli (spirals), rigatoni (hollow ridged tubes), farfalle (bows) and penne (quills), will more easily hold thicker, meaty and substantial sauces. Pasta sheets and tubes, such as lasagne and cannelloni, are also suited to rich, thick sauces with which they are baked in the oven. The recipes in this book suggest particular pasta shapes, but you can substitute your own favourites.

The book is divided into four sections, according to the main ingredients of the sauce – Meat & Poultry, Cheese & Cream, Fish & Shellfish, and Vegetables. Some are familiar classics, such as Pasta with Bolognese Sauce, Spaghetti alla Carbonara, Tagliatelle with Gorgonzola Sauce and Pasta Napoletana. Others offer a more unusual and adventurous combination of flavours and textures. Try Linguine with Clams, Leeks and Tomatoes, Fusilli with Turkey, Pasta with Courgette and Walnut Sauce or Greek Pasta with Avocado Sauce; they will soon become firm family favourites, too. Most of the sauces are quick and easy to make – some taking only a few minutes. A few are a little more complicated and time-consuming, but would be a perfect choice for when friends visit.

Types of Pasta

There are thought to be at least 200 different pasta shapes – with about three times as many different names. New shapes and "designer" pasta are being produced all the time. Moreover, the same shape may have a different name in different regions of Italy.

Fresh and dried pasta

Perhaps more importantly, pasta can be categorized as dried and fresh. Many different shapes of dried pasta are readily available from supermarkets. It is probably not worth buying fresh unfilled pasta unless you have access to a really excellent Italian delicatessen. Buying fresh filled pasta, however, is worthwhile.

Basic plain pasta, whether fresh or dried, is made from durum flour, olive oil and eggs. Additional ingredients may colour it. Green, flavoured with spinach,

tagliatelle

linguine

ravioli

rigatoni

fusilli

macaroni

tortellini

spirali

canneroni

castiglioni

spaghetti tricolore

fusilli tricolore

curly lasagne

is the commonest variation. Red pasta is flavoured with tomatoes and black pasta with cuttlefish ink.

Wholemeal pasta may be substituted for ordinary pasta. Made with both wholemeal and plain white flour, it has a firmer texture and contains more fibre.

gomiti
rigati

orecchiette

spaghetti

penne

fusilli col buco

Cooking Pasta

The secret to cooking perfect pasta is not to overcook it. In Italy it is cooked until it is al dente ("to the tooth"), that is just tender, but still firm to the bite. Make sure that you use a big enough saucepan to hold plenty of boiling water. Allow 3 litres/5¼ pints/12½ cups for each 450g/1lb of pasta.

1 Bring a large saucepan of lightly salted water to the boil.

2 Add 15ml/1 tbsp olive oil. This will prevent the water from boiling over and also stop the pasta from sticking together.

3 Add the pasta to the pan and stir with a wooden spoon to separate. Bring the water back to a rolling boil and cook until the pasta is just tender, but still firm to the bite.

4 Drain in a colander and toss thoroughly in olive oil, butter or your chosen sauce, using two forks to ensure that it is well coated. Alternatively, transfer to a dish and pour the sauce on top.

COOKING TIMES

Time from the moment the water returns to a rolling boil after you have added the pasta.

Fresh unfilled pasta:	2–3 minutes
Dried unfilled pasta:	8–12 minutes
Fresh filled pasta:	8–10 minutes
Dried filled pasta:	15–20 minutes

These are only guidelines and you should check while the pasta is boiling to avoid overcooking.

Herbs

These are one of the important ingredients in any sauce. It is always better to use fresh rather than dried herbs if possible. However, some dried herbs may be used successfully. As their flavour is concentrated, use only half the quantity specified in the recipe for fresh herbs. Some herbs, particularly the delicate ones, are better frozen than dried.

Choosing herbs
When buying fresh herbs, look for clean, unblemished leaves with a pleasant aroma and a good colour. Depending on the variety, they may be chopped finely or coarsely, torn into pieces or left whole in sprigs. A fresh sprig also makes an attractive garnish. Ideally, fresh herbs should be used immediately after cutting, but this is not always possible. Most can be stored for a short while in the refrigerator with their stems in a jar of water and covered with a plastic bag.

Basil
This is the classic herb for pasta sauces. It has a warm, pungent aroma and flavour, and the leaves are soft and shiny. They are best torn by hand, rather than chopped, as this retains more flavour. The most frequently available type of basil is also known as sweet basil. Other varieties include Neapolitana, which has large, crinkled leaves and a very strong flavour that makes it perfect for pesto. There are also several purple varieties. Basil is the ideal herb for tomato sauces, delicate ricotta cheese fillings, and fish and poultry sauces. It is, of course, a main ingredient in pesto and can simply be used with garlic and olive oil to dress freshly cooked pasta for a quick and easy lunch. It is not suitable for hearty meat sauces, which will drown its flavour. Dried basil is a poor substitute for fresh, lacking in both pungency and colour. If you cannot obtain fresh basil, use a spoonful of ready-made pesto sauce instead.

Bay leaves
The bay is a member of the laurel family and, as it is evergreen, fresh leaves are available all year. They are firm and shiny with a dull underside. Dried bay leaves are a satisfactory substitute. Strongly fragrant, bay leaves are used to flavour meat sauces and béchamel or white sauces in baked dishes.

Coriander
Similar to flat leaf parsley in appearance, coriander has an intense fragrance and delicious flavour. It is usually used roughly chopped and fresh sprigs make a very attractive garnish. It goes well with most ingredients, including poultry and meat.

Dill
The feathery leaves have a distinctive, aniseed-like flavour. Traditionally used to flavour fish sauces, it also goes well with cream cheese and cucumber.

Marjoram and oregano
These herbs belong to the same family; oregano is also known as wild marjoram. It has a stronger flavour than sweet marjoram. They are among the most popular herbs in the Italian kitchen. They keep their flavour well when dried. Both go well with tomato and egg sauces, as well as meat, fish and poultry. When in flower, they make an unusual and appealing garnish.

Mint
There are many different varieties of mint. Some, like apple or pineapple mint, have an overlying flavour. Mint is a popular herb in Italy for using with fish.

Parsley
This a very versatile, almost all-purpose herb. It has a fresh, "green" taste that goes well with meat, poultry, fish and vegetable sauces. A delicious pesto sauce can be made using parsley instead of basil. There are two varieties, curly and flat leaf. There is little difference in the flavour. Curly parsley is usually finely chopped, while the flat leaf variety is better coarsely chopped.

Rosemary
The dark green, needle-like leaves of rosemary are intensely aromatic with a very powerful flavour, so it should be used with discretion. The resinous oils ensure that dried rosemary is almost as pungent as fresh. It is traditionally used to flavour lamb, but also goes well with pork. The needles are extremely tough, so they should be very finely chopped.

Sage
Together with basil, oregano and marjoram, sage is one of the most popular Italian herbs. Fresh sage is strongly flavoured and very aromatic. Dried sage is not a very satisfactory substitute and tends to become dusty. Sage goes well with strongly flavoured ingredients, such as meat, garlic, tomatoes and Gorgonzola cheese. It is frequently used in stuffed pasta dishes from the Emilia-Romagna region. There are many varieties, including ones with variegated leaves.

thyme

rosemary

basil

sage

flat leaf parsley

dill

coriander

mint

oregano

Thyme
The tiny, grey-green leaves are extremely pungent and very aromatic, as they contain highly concentrated, volatile essential oils. There are many varieties of thyme, ranging from wild thyme to spicy lemon and orange. Common thyme goes well with meat sauces, and lemon thyme is delicious with fish and seafood.

Chopping herbs
For finely chopped herbs, pull the leaves off the stems and pile them together on a chopping board. With one hand, hold down the point of a sharp knife to act as a pivot, and chop backwards and forwards across the leaves. Alternatively, you can use a special herb chopper called a mezzaluna. This double-handled blade is simply rocked over the pile of leaves from side to side.

For coarsely chopped herbs, hold the leaves in one hand bunched against the blade of a sharp knife. Chop with the knife against your fingers – with care.

Some herbs are most easily prepared by snipping them with kitchen scissors. Basil leaves are usually coarsely torn by hand.

Basic Sauce Ingredients

There is no need to buy expensive and sophisticated ingredients to make delicious pasta sauces. However, it is worth taking note of some typically Italian or other especially useful ingredients.

Clams
There are many different varieties of clams found in the coastal waters of almost every continent. The tiny variety, known in Italy as *vongole*, are best for pasta sauces. If fresh clams are unavailable, you could substitute fresh cockles or clams canned in brine.

Dolcelatte
This blue-veined, semi-soft Italian cheese has a delicate, piquant flavour and a creamy texture. It is used in sauces and pasta fillings.

Feta
This Greek cheese is traditionally made from ewe's milk, but now is more frequently made from cow's milk. It is crumbly with a bland, slightly salty flavour, as it is preserved in brine. It is usually sold vacuum packed and is produced by many other countries as well.

Gorgonzola
One of the oldest blue-veined cheeses in the world, Gorgonzola is semi-soft, creamy and piquant in flavour. It should have a distinctive but not bitter smell.

Italian sausages
These are highly seasoned and meaty, ranging in size from about 50g/2oz to 1kg/2¼lb. Varieties include *cervellata*, a pork sausage flavoured with Parmesan cheese and saffron, and *cotechino*, pork flavoured with white wine, cloves and cinnamon. Squeeze the meat

from the casing to make easy sauces and stuffings.

Mediterranean prawns
About 20–23 cm/8–9 inches long, these have more flavour than smaller varieties. They are available raw and cooked. Make sure frozen prawns are fully thawed.

Mussels
Fresh mussels are best, and they should be cooked on the day of purchase. Frozen cooked mussels may be used as a substitute.

Nuts
Pistachios and walnuts are excellent for colouring and flavouring a variety of sauces.

Olives
Olives are used to add richness to sauces. Black olives have a stronger flavour than green.

Onions
Used to add a strong undertone to sauces made with meat, fish and vegetables, onions are essential in the Italian kitchen. Red onions have a mild flavour and look attractive. Spanish onions are sweeter than other varieties.

Pancetta
This Italian bacon adds flavour to sauces and is a traditional ingredient in such classic recipes as spaghetti alla carbonara. It may be smoked or unsmoked, sliced or in a single piece. If you cannot obtain it, substitute streaky bacon, but the flavour will be less powerful.

Parmesan cheese
This hard cheese comes from a specified area in north-central Italy and the rind is always stamped

black olives

pancetta

smoked salmon

spina

Mediterran
prawns

Italian sausages

with *Parmigiano Reggiano* as a guarantee of its origin. It has a grainy texture and a fragrant flavour. Grated Parmesan or thin shavings are sprinkled over many pasta sauces just before serving or at the table. It is better to buy Parmesan cheese in a single piece and grate it freshly as required.

Peppers
Available in a variety of colours, peppers are a tasty and colourful

feta

Parmesan

red and yellow peppers

Gorgonzola

dolcelatte

onions

mussels

ricotta

pistachios

pine nuts

clams

pear tomatoes

cherry tomatoes

plum tomato

walnuts

addition to pasta sauces. Red, yellow and orange peppers are sweeter than green ones.

Pine nuts
Small, cream-coloured and very oily, pine nuts are essential for making pesto sauce. They do not keep well.

Ricotta
This Italian whey cheese is creamy and white with a smooth, soft

texture and a bland, slightly sweet flavour. It is very versatile and used with ingredients, such as spinach and nuts, for pasta stuffings.

Smoked salmon
Thinly sliced smoked salmon is a quick and easy addition both to sauces and pasta stuffings.

Spinach
The deep green, iron-rich leaves are used to colour pasta, as well as for

making sauces and stuffings. Young spinach leaves are the most tender.

Tomatoes
Buy fresh tomatoes that are really ripe. Typically Italian, plum tomatoes have a concentrated flavour and less watery flesh than many other varieties, making them ideal for pasta sauces. Miniature or cherry tomatoes are also excellent in pasta sauces. Canned plum tomatoes are a useful stand-by.

MEAT &
POULTRY
SAUCES

~

Pasta with Bolognese Sauce

Traditional Bolognese sauce contains chicken livers to add richness, but you can leave them out and replace with an equal quantity of minced beef.

INGREDIENTS

Serves 4–6

75g/3oz pancetta or bacon

115g/4oz chicken livers

50g/2oz/4 tbsp butter, plus extra for
   tossing the pasta

1 onion, finely chopped

1 carrot, diced

1 celery stick, finely chopped

225g/8oz/2 cups lean minced beef

30ml/2 tbsp tomato purée

120ml/4fl oz/½ cup white wine

200ml/7fl oz/scant 1 cup beef stock
   or water

freshly grated nutmeg

450g/1lb tagliatelle, spaghetti or fettuccine

salt and ground black pepper

freshly grated Parmesan cheese, to serve

1 Dice the pancetta or bacon. Trim the chicken livers, removing any fat or gristle and any "green" bits which will be bitter if left on. Roughly chop the livers.

2 Melt 50g/2oz/4 tbsp butter in a saucepan and add the bacon. Cook for 2-3 minutes until just beginning to brown. Then add the onion, carrot and celery and brown these too.

3 Stir in the beef and brown over a high heat, breaking it up with a spoon. Add the chicken livers and cook for 2-3 minutes. Add the tomato purée with the wine and stock or water. Season well with salt, pepper and nutmeg. Bring to the boil, cover and simmer for 35 minutes.

4 Cook the pasta in plenty of boiling salted water according to the instructions on the packet or until *al dente*. Drain well and toss with the extra butter. Toss the meat sauce with the pasta and serve with plenty of grated Parmesan cheese.

Pasta Spirals with Chicken and Tomato

A recipe for a speedy supper – serve this dish with a mixed bean salad.

INGREDIENTS

Serves 4

15ml/1 tbsp olive oil
1 onion, chopped
1 carrot, chopped
50g/2oz sun-dried tomatoes in olive oil, drained weight
1 garlic clove, chopped
400g/14oz can chopped tomatoes, drained
15ml/1 tbsp tomato purée
150ml/¼ pint/⅔ cup chicken stock
350g/12oz fusilli
225g/8oz chicken, diagonally sliced
salt and ground black pepper
fresh mint sprigs, to garnish

3 Stir the garlic, tomatoes, tomato purée and stock into the onions and carrots and bring to the boil. Simmer for 10 minutes, stirring occasionally.

4 Cook the pasta in plenty of boiling salted water according to the instructions on the packet.

5 Pour the sauce into a blender or food processor and process until smooth.

6 Return the sauce to the pan and stir in the sun-dried tomatoes and chicken. Bring back to the boil and then simmer for 10 minutes until the chicken is cooked. Adjust the seasoning, if necessary.

7 Drain the pasta thoroughly and toss in the sauce. Serve at once, garnished with sprigs of fresh mint.

1 Heat the oil in a large frying pan and fry the onion and carrot for 5 minutes, stirring the vegetables occasionally.

2 Chop the sun-dried tomatoes and set aside until needed.

Spirali with Smoky Bacon Sauce

A wonderful sauce to prepare in mid-summer when the tomatoes are ripe and sweet.

INGREDIENTS

Serves 4

900g/2lb ripe tomatoes

6 rashers smoked streaky bacon

50g/2oz/4 tbsp butter

1 onion, chopped

15ml/1 tbsp chopped fresh oregano or
     5ml/1 tsp dried

450g/1lb pasta, any variety

salt and ground black pepper

freshly grated Parmesan cheese, to serve

1 Plunge the tomatoes into boiling water for 1 minute, then into cold water. Slip off the skins. Halve the tomatoes, remove the seeds and cores and roughly chop the flesh.

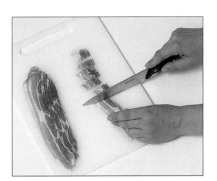

2 Remove the rind from the streaky bacon and roughly chop the meat.

3 Melt the butter in a saucepan and add the bacon. Fry until lightly browned, then add the onion and cook gently for 5 minutes until softened. Add the tomatoes, salt, pepper and oregano. Simmer gently for 10 minutes.

4 Cook the pasta in plenty of boiling salted water according to the instructions on the packet. Drain well and toss with the sauce. Serve with plenty of freshly grated Parmesan cheese.

Spaghetti with Bacon and Tomato Sauce

This substantial sauce is a meal in itself, so serve it up as a warming winter supper.

Serves 4

15ml/1 tbsp olive oil

225g/8oz smoked streaky bacon, rinded and roughly chopped

250g/9oz spaghetti

5ml/1 tsp chilli powder

1 quantity Classic Tomato Sauce (see Curly Lasagne with Classic Tomato Sauce)

salt and ground black pepper

roughly chopped fresh flat leaf parsley, to garnish

1 Heat the oil in large frying pan and fry the bacon for about 10 minutes, stirring occasionally until crisp and golden.

2 Cook the pasta following the instructions on the packet, until *al dente*.

3 Add the chilli powder to the bacon and cook for 2 minutes. Stir in the tomato sauce and bring to the boil. Cover and simmer for 10 minutes. Season with salt and pepper to taste.

4 Drain the pasta thoroughly and toss it together with the sauce. Serve garnished with the roughly chopped fresh parsley.

Tagliatelle with Pea and Ham Sauce

A colourful sauce, this is ideal served with crusty Italian or French bread.

Serves 4

350g/12oz tagliatelle

225g/8oz/1½ cups shelled peas

300ml/½ pint/1¼ cups single cream

50g/2oz/⅓ cup freshly grated fontina cheese

75g/3oz Parma ham, sliced into strips

salt and ground black pepper

1 Cook the pasta following the instructions on the packet until *al dente*.

2 Plunge the peas into a pan of boiling salted water and cook for about 7 minutes or until tender. Drain and set aside.

3 Place the cream and half the fontina cheese in a small saucepan and heat gently, stirring constantly until heated through.

4 Drain the pasta thoroughly and turn it into a large serving bowl. Toss together the pasta, ham and peas and pour on the sauce. Add the remaining cheese and season with salt and pepper to taste.

Rigatoni with Spicy Sausage

This is really a cheat's Bolognese sauce using the wonderful fresh spicy sausages sold in every good Italian delicatessen.

INGREDIENTS

Serves 4

450g/1lb fresh spicy Italian sausage

30ml/2 tbsp olive oil

1 onion, chopped

450ml/¾ pint/1¾ cups passata

150ml/¼ pint/⅔ cup dry red wine

6 sun-dried tomatoes in oil, drained

450g/1lb rigatoni or similar pasta

salt and ground black pepper

freshly grated Parmesan cheese, to serve

1 Squeeze the sausages out of their skins into a bowl and break up the meat.

2 Heat the oil in a medium saucepan and add the onion. Cook for 5 minutes until soft and golden. Stir in the sausagemeat, browning it all over and breaking up the lumps with a wooden spoon. Pour in the passata and the wine. Bring to the boil.

3 Slice the sun-dried tomatoes and add to the sauce. Simmer for 3 minutes until reduced, stirring occasionally. Season.

4 Cook the pasta in plenty of boiling salted water according to the instructions on the packet. Drain well and top with the sauce. Serve with Parmesan cheese.

Spicy Beef

If you are hungry and only have a few minutes to spare for cooking, this colourful and healthy dish is an excellent choice.

INGREDIENTS

Serves 4

15ml/1 tbsp oil

450g/1lb/4 cups minced beef

2.5cm/1in piece fresh root ginger, sliced

5ml/1 tsp Chinese five-spice powder

1 red chilli, sliced

50g/2oz mange-touts

1 red pepper, seeded and chopped

1 carrot, sliced

115g/4oz beansprouts

15ml/1 tbsp sesame oil

cooked Chinese egg noodles, to serve

3 Add the mange-touts, the seeded and chopped red pepper and sliced carrot and cook for a further 3 minutes, stirring the mixture continuously.

4 Add the beansprouts and sesame oil and cook for a final 2 minutes. Serve immediately with Chinese egg noodles.

1 Heat the oil in a wok until almost smoking. Add the minced beef and cook for about 3 minutes, stirring all the time.

2 Add the ginger, Chinese five-spice powder and chilli. Cook for 1 minute.

Tagliatelle with Parma Ham and Asparagus

A stunning sauce, this is worth every effort to serve at a dinner party.

INGREDIENTS

Serves 4

350g/12oz tagliatelle
25g/1oz/2 tbsp butter
15ml/1 tbsp olive oil
225g/8oz asparagus tips
1 garlic clove, chopped
115g/4oz Parma ham, sliced into strips
30ml/2 tbsp chopped fresh sage
150ml/¼ pint/⅔ cup single cream
115g/4oz/1 cup grated chive-and-onion
   double Gloucester cheese
115g/4oz/1 cup grated Gruyère cheese
salt and ground black pepper
fresh sage sprigs, to garnish

1 Cook the pasta in plenty of boiling salted water according to the instructions on the packet.

2 Melt the butter and oil in a frying pan and gently fry the asparagus tips for about 5 minutes, stirring occasionally, until they are almost tender.

3 Stir in the garlic and Parma ham and fry for 1 minute.

4 Stir in the chopped sage and fry for a further 1 minute.

5 Pour in the cream and bring the mixture to the boil.

6 Add the cheeses and simmer gently, stirring occasionally, until thoroughly melted. Season.

7 Drain the pasta thoroughly and toss with the sauce to coat. Serve immediately, garnished with fresh sage sprigs.

Peasant Bolognese

A spicy version of a popular dish. Worcestershire sauce and chorizo sausages add an extra element to this perfect family standby.

INGREDIENTS

Serves 4

15ml/1 tbsp oil

225g/8oz/2 cups minced beef

1 onion, chopped

5ml/1 tsp chilli powder

15ml/1 tbsp Worcestershire sauce

25g/1oz/2 tbsp plain flour

150ml/¼ pint/⅔ cup beef stock

4 chorizo sausages

50g/2oz baby sweetcorn

200g/7oz can chopped tomatoes

15ml/1 tbsp chopped fresh basil

salt and ground black pepper

cooked spaghetti, to serve

fresh basil, to garnish

1 Heat the oil in a large pan and fry the minced beef for 5 minutes. Add the onion and chilli powder and cook for a further 3 minutes.

COOK'S TIP

Make up the Bolognese sauce and freeze in conveniently sized portions for up to two months.

2 Stir in the Worcestershire sauce and flour. Cook for 1 minute before pouring in the stock.

3 Slice the chirozo sausages and halve the corn lengthways.

4 Stir in the sausages, tomatoes, sweetcorn and chopped basil. Season well and bring to the boil. Reduce the heat and simmer for 30 minutes. Serve with spaghetti, garnished with fresh basil.

Tagliatelle with Chicken and Herb Sauce

Serve this delicious dish with its wine-flavoured sauce and a fresh green salad.

INGREDIENTS

Serves 4

30ml/2 tbsp olive oil

1 red onion, cut into wedges

350g/12oz tagliatelle

1 garlic clove, chopped

350g/12oz chicken, diced

300ml/½ pint/1¼ cups dry vermouth

45ml/3 tbsp chopped fresh mixed herbs

150ml/¼ pint/⅔ cup fromage frais

salt and ground black pepper

shredded fresh mint, to garnish

1 Heat the oil in a large frying pan and fry the red onion for 10 minutes until softened and the layers have separated.

2 Cook the pasta in plenty of boiling salted water according to the instructions on the packet.

3 Add the garlic and chicken to the frying pan and fry for 10 minutes, stirring occasionally, until the chicken is browned all over and cooked through.

4 Pour in the vermouth, bring to boiling point and boil rapidly until reduced by about half.

5 Stir in the herbs, fromage frais and seasoning and heat through gently, but do not boil.

6 Drain the pasta thoroughly and toss with the sauce to coat. Serve immediately, garnished with shredded fresh mint.

Spaghetti in a Cream and Bacon Sauce

This is a light and creamy sauce flavoured with bacon and lightly cooked eggs.

Serves 4

350g/12oz spaghetti

15ml/1 tbsp olive oil

1 onion, chopped

115g/4oz rindless streaky bacon or
   pancetta, diced

1 garlic clove, chopped

3 eggs

300ml/½ pint/1¼ cups double cream

50g/2oz Parmesan cheese

chopped fresh basil, to garnish

1 Cook the pasta in plenty of boiling salted water according to the instructions on the packet.

2 Heat the oil in a frying pan and fry the onion and bacon or pancetta for 10 minutes, until softened. Stir in the garlic and fry for a further 2 minutes, stirring occasionally.

3 Meanwhile, beat the eggs in a bowl, then stir in the cream and seasoning. Grate the Parmesan cheese and stir into the egg and cream mixture.

4 Stir the cream mixture into the onion and bacon or pancetta and cook over a low heat for a few minutes, stirring constantly, until heated through. Season to taste.

5 Drain the pasta thoroughly and turn into a large serving dish. Pour over the sauce and toss to coat. Serve immediately, garnished with chopped fresh basil.

Rigatoni with Garlic Crumbs

A hot and spicy dish – halve the quantity of chilli if you like a milder flavour. The bacon is an optional addition; you can leave it out if you are cooking for vegetarians.

INGREDIENTS

Serves 4–6

45ml/3 tbsp olive oil

2 shallots, chopped

8 rashers streaky bacon, chopped (optional)

10ml/2 tsp crushed dried red chillies

400g/14oz can chopped tomatoes with garlic and herbs

6 slices white bread

115g/4oz/½ cup butter

2 garlic cloves, chopped

450g/1lb rigatoni

salt and ground black pepper

1 Heat the oil in a medium saucepan and fry the shallots and bacon, if using, gently for 6–8 minutes until golden. Add the dried chillies and chopped tomatoes, half-cover and simmer for 20 minutes.

2 Meanwhile, cut the crusts off the bread and discard them. Reduce the bread to crumbs in a blender or food processor.

3 Heat the butter in a frying pan, add the garlic and bread-crumbs and stir-fry until golden and crisp. (Don't let the crumbs catch and burn or the final result will be ruined.)

4 Cook the pasta in plenty of boiling salted water according to the instructions on the packet, until *al dente*. Drain well.

5 Toss the pasta with the tomato sauce and divide among four or six warmed serving plates.

6 Sprinkle with the crumbs and serve immediately.

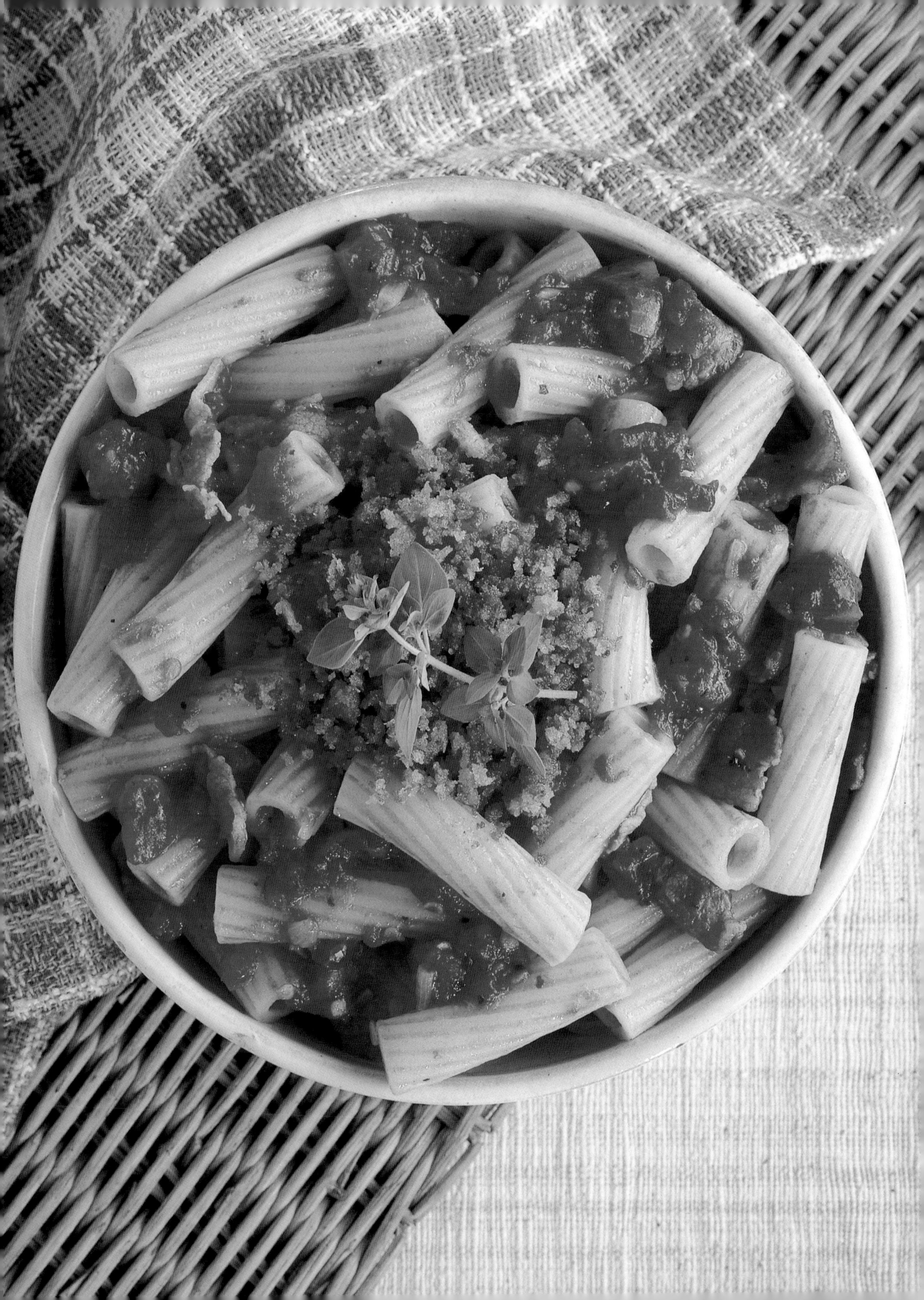

Pasta Twists with Classic Meat Sauce

This is a rich meat sauce which is ideal to serve with all types of pasta. The sauce definitely improves if kept overnight in the fridge. This allows the flavours time to mature.

INGREDIENTS

Serves 4

450g/1lb/4 cups minced beef

115g/4oz smoked streaky beacon, rinded and chopped

1 onion, chopped

2 celery sticks, chopped

15ml/1 tbsp plain flour

150ml/¼ pint/⅔ cup chicken stock or water

45ml/3 tbsp tomato purée

1 garlic clove, chopped

45ml/3 tbsp chopped fresh mixed herbs, such as oregano, parsley, marjoram and chives or 15ml/1 tbsp dried mixed herbs

15ml/1 tbsp redcurrant jelly

350g/12oz pasta twists, such as spirali

salt and ground black pepper

chopped oregano, to garnish

1 Heat a large saucepan and fry the beef and bacon for about 10 minutes, stirring occasionally until browned.

2 Add the chopped onion and celery and cook for 2 minutes, stirring occasionally.

COOK'S TIP

The redcurrant jelly helps to draw out the flavour of the tomato purée. You can use a sweet mint jelly or chutney instead, if you like.

3 Stir in the flour and cook for 2 minutes, stirring constantly.

4 Pour in the stock or water and bring to the boil.

5 Stir in the tomato purée, garlic, herbs, redcurrant jelly and seasoning. Bring to the boil, cover and simmer for about 30 minutes.

6 Cook the pasta in plenty of boiling salted water according to the instructions on the packet. Drain thoroughly and turn into a large serving dish. Pour over the sauce and toss to coat. Serve the pasta immediately, garnished with chopped fresh oregano.

Pasta Tubes with Meat and Cheese Sauce

The two sauces complement each other perfectly in this wonderfully flavoursome dish.

INGREDIENTS

Serves 4

350g/12oz rigatoni
salt and ground black pepper
fresh basil sprigs, to garnish

For the meat sauce
15ml/1 tbsp olive oil
350g/12oz/3 cups minced beef
1 onion, chopped
1 garlic clove, chopped
400g/14oz can chopped tomatoes
15ml/1 tbsp dried mixed herbs
30ml/2 tbsp tomato purée

For the cheese sauce
50g/2oz/¼ cup butter
50g/2oz/½ cup plain flour
450ml/¾ pint/1¾ cups milk
2 egg yolks
50g/2oz/½ cup freshly grated
   Parmesan cheese

5 Add the egg yolks, cheese and seasoning and stir until the sauce is well blended.

6 Preheat the grill. Meanwhile, cook the pasta in plenty of boiling salted water according to the instructions on the packet. Drain thoroughly and turn into a large mixing bowl. Pour over the meat sauce and toss to coat.

7 Divide the pasta among four flameproof dishes. Spoon over the cheese sauce and place under the grill until brown. Serve immediately, garnished with fresh basil.

1 To make the meat sauce, heat the oil in a large frying pan and fry the beef for 10 minutes, stirring occasionally until browned. Add the onion and cook for 5 minutes, stirring occasionally.

2 Stir in the garlic, tomatoes, herbs and tomato purée. Bring to the boil, cover, and simmer for about 30 minutes.

3 Meanwhile, to make the cheese sauce, melt the butter in a small saucepan, then stir in the flour and cook for 2 minutes, stirring constantly.

4 Remove the pan from the heat and gradually stir in the milk. Return the pan to the heat and bring to the boil, stirring occasionally, until thickened.

Spaghetti alla Carbonara

It has been said that this dish was originally cooked by Italian coal miners or charcoal-burners, hence the name "carbonara". The secret of its creamy sauce is not to overcook the egg.

INGREDIENTS

Serves 4

175g/6oz unsmoked streaky bacon

1 garlic clove, chopped

3 eggs

450g/1lb spaghetti

60ml/4 tbsp freshly grated
   Parmesan cheese

salt and ground black pepper

1 Dice the bacon and place in a medium saucepan. Fry in its own fat with the garlic until brown. Keep warm until needed.

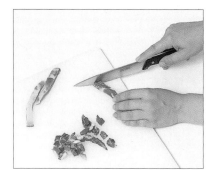

2 Whisk the eggs together in a mixing bowl.

3 Cook the spaghetti in plenty of boiling salted water according to the instructions on the packet or until *al dente*. Drain well.

4 Quickly turn the spaghetti into the pan with the bacon and stir in the eggs, a little salt, lots of pepper and half the cheese. Toss well to mix. The eggs should half-cook in the heat from the pasta. Serve in warmed bowls with the remaining Parmesan cheese sprinkled over each portion.

Penne with Sausage and Parmesan Sauce

Spicy sausage tossed in a cheesy tomato sauce is delicious served on a bed of cooked pasta.

INGREDIENTS

Serves 4

350g/12oz penne
450g/1lb ripe tomatoes
30ml/2 tbsp olive oil
225g/8oz chorizo sausage,
    diagonally sliced
1 garlic clove, chopped
30ml/2 tbsp chopped fresh flat leaf parsley
grated rind of 1 lemon
50g/2oz/½ cup freshly grated
    Parmesan cheese
salt and ground black pepper
finely chopped fresh flat leaf parsley,
    to garnish

1 Cook the pasta in plenty of boiling salted water according to the instructions on the packet.

2 Slash the bottoms of the tomatoes with a knife, making a cross. Place in a large bowl, cover with boiling water and leave to stand for 45 seconds. Plunge into cold water for 30 seconds, then peel off the skins and roughly chop the flesh.

3 Heat the oil in a frying pan and fry the sliced chorizo sausage for 5 minutes, stirring from time to time, until browned.

4 Add the chopped tomatoes, garlic, parsley and grated lemon rind. Heat through gently, stirring, for 1 minute.

5 Add the grated Parmesan cheese and season to taste.

6 Drain the pasta well through a colander and toss it with the sauce to coat. Serve immediately, garnished with finely chopped fresh flat leaf parsley.

Noodles with Pancetta and Mushrooms

Porcini mushrooms give this sauce a wonderful depth.

INGREDIENTS

Serves 2–4

25g/1oz dried Italian mushrooms (porcini)

175ml/6fl oz/¾ cup warm water

900g/2lb tomatoes, peeled, seeded and chopped or drained canned tomatoes

1.5ml/¼ tsp dried hot chilli flakes

45ml/3 tbsp olive oil

4 slices pancetta or rashers unsmoked back bacon, cut into thin strips

1 large garlic clove, finely chopped

350g/12oz tagliatelle or fettuccine

salt and ground black pepper

freshly grated Parmesan cheese, to serve

1 Put the mushrooms in a bowl and cover with the warm water. Leave to soak for 20 minutes.

2 Meanwhile, put the tomatoes in a saucepan with the chilli flakes and seasoning. If using canned tomatoes, crush them coarsely with a fork or potato masher. Bring to the boil, reduce the heat and simmer for about 30–40 minutes, until reduced to 750ml/1¼ pints/3 cups. Stir from time to time to prevent sticking.

3 When the mushrooms have finished soaking, lift them out and squeeze the remaining liquid over the bowl; set aside.

4 Carefully pour the soaking liquid into the tomatoes through a muslin-lined sieve. Simmer the tomatoes for a further 15 minutes.

5 Meanwhile, heat 30ml/2 tbsp of the oil in a frying pan. Add the strips of pancetta or bacon and fry until golden but not crisp. Add the garlic and mushrooms and fry for 3 minutes, stirring. Set aside.

6 Cook the pasta in plenty of boiling salted water until just *al dente*.

7 Add the bacon and mushroom mixture to the tomato sauce and mix well. Season with salt and ground black pepper.

8 Drain the pasta and return to the pan. Add the remaining oil and toss to coat the strands. Divide among hot plates, spoon the sauce on top and serve with freshly grated Parmesan cheese.

Pasta Spirals with Pepperoni and Tomato

A warming supper dish, perfect for a cold winter's night. All types of sausage are suitable, but if using raw sausages, add them with the onion to cook thoroughly.

INGREDIENTS

Serves 4

1 onion

1 red pepper

1 green pepper

30ml/2 tbsp olive oil, plus extra for
   tossing the pasta

800g/1¾ lb canned chopped tomatoes

30ml/2 tbsp tomato purée

10ml/2 tsp paprika

175g/6oz pepperoni or chorizo sausage

45ml/3 tbsp chopped fresh parsley

450g/1lb pasta spirals, such as fusilli

salt and ground black pepper

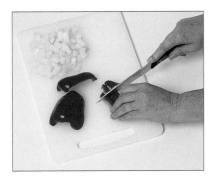

1 Chop the onion. Halve, core and seed the peppers. Cut the flesh into dice.

2 Heat the oil in a medium saucepan, add the onion and cook for 2–3 minutes until beginning to colour. Stir in the peppers, tomatoes, tomato purée and paprika, bring to the boil and simmer uncovered for about 15–20 minutes until reduced and thickened.

3 Slice the pepperoni or chorizo and stir into the sauce with 30ml/2 tbsp of the chopped parsley. Season to taste with salt and pepper.

4 While the sauce is simmering, cook the pasta in plenty of boiling salted water according to the instructions on the packet. Drain well. Toss the pasta with the remaining parsley in a little extra olive oil. Divide among four warmed bowls and top with sauce.

Pasta with Devilled Kidneys

Ask your butcher to prepare the kidneys for you if you prefer.

INGREDIENTS

Serves 4

8–10 lambs' kidneys

15ml/1 tbsp sunflower oil

25g/1oz/2 tbsp butter

10ml/2 tsp paprika

5–10ml/1–2 tsp mild grainy mustard

salt, to taste

chopped fresh parsley, to garnish

225g/8oz fresh pasta, to serve

1 Cut the kidneys in half and neatly cut out the white cores with scissors. Cut the kidneys again if very large.

2 Heat the oil and butter together. Add the kidneys and cook, turning frequently, for about 2 minutes. Blend the paprika and mustard together with a little salt and stir into the pan.

3 Continue cooking the kidneys, basting frequently, for about a further 3–4 minutes.

4 Cook the pasta for about 10–12 minutes, or according to the instructions on the packet. Serve the kidneys and their sauce, topped with the chopped fresh parsley, and accompanied by the pasta.

Golden-topped Pasta

When it comes to the children helping you to plan the menus, this is the sort of dish that always wins hands down. It is also perfect for "padding out" if you have to feed eight instead of four people.

INGREDIENTS

Serves 4–6

225g/8oz dried pasta shells or spirals

115g/4oz/⅔ cup chopped cooked ham, beef or turkey

350g/12oz par-cooked mixed vegetables, such as carrots, cauliflower, beans, etc

a little oil

For the cheese sauce

25g/1oz/2 tbsp butter

25g/1oz/2 tbsp plain flour

300ml/½ pint/1¼ cups milk

175g/6oz/1½ cups grated Cheddar cheese

5–10ml/1–2 tsp mustard

salt and ground black pepper

1 Cook the pasta according to the instructions on the packet. Drain and place in a flameproof dish with the chopped meat, the vegetables and 5–10ml/1–2 tsp oil.

2 Melt the butter in a saucepan, stir in the flour and cook for 1 minute, stirring. Remove from the heat and gradually stir in the milk. Return to the heat, bring to the boil, stirring and cook for 2 minutes. Add half the cheese, the mustard and seasoning to taste.

3 Spoon the sauce over the meat and vegetables. Sprinkle with the rest of the cheese and grill quickly until golden and bubbling.

Cannelloni with Spinach and Cheese Sauce

This version of a classic Italian dish introduces a variety of vegetables which are topped with a traditional cheese sauce.

INGREDIENTS

Serves 4

8 cannelloni tubes

115g/4oz spinach

For the filling

15ml/1 tbsp oil

175g/6oz/1½ cups minced beef

2 garlic cloves, crushed

25g/1oz/2 tbsp plain flour

120ml/4fl oz/½ cup beef stock

1 small carrot, finely chopped

1 small yellow courgette, chopped

salt and ground black pepper

For the sauce

25g/1oz/2 tbsp butter

25g/1oz/2 tbsp plain flour

250ml/8fl oz/1 cup milk

50g/2oz/½ cup freshly grated
 Parmesan cheese

1 Preheat the oven to 180°C/ 350°F/Gas 4. For the filling, heat the oil in a large pan. Add the minced beef and garlic. Cook for 5 minutes.

2 Add the flour and cook for a further 1 minute. Slowly stir in the stock and bring to the boil.

3 Add the carrot and courgette. Season. Cook for 10 minutes.

4 Spoon the mince mixture into the cannelloni tubes and place in an ovenproof dish.

5 Blanch the spinach in boiling water for 3 minutes. Drain well and place on top of the cannelloni tubes in the dish.

6 For the sauce melt the butter in a pan. Add the flour and cook for 1 minute. Pour in the milk, add the grated cheese and season well. Bring to the boil, stirring all the time. Pour over the cannelloni and spinach and bake for 30 minutes. Serve with tomatoes and a crisp green salad, if liked.

Penne with Chicken and Ham Sauce

A meal in itself, this colourful pasta sauce is perfect for lunch or supper.

INGREDIENTS

Serves 4

350g/12oz penne

25g/1oz/2 tbsp butter

1 onion, chopped

1 garlic clove, chopped

1 bay leaf

450ml/¾ pint/1¾ cups dry white wine

150ml/¼ pint/⅔ cup crème fraîche

225g/8oz cooked chicken, skinned, boned and diced

115g/4oz cooked lean ham, diced

115g/4oz Gouda cheese, grated

15ml/1 tbsp chopped fresh mint

salt and ground black pepper

finely shredded fresh mint, to garnish

1 Cook the pasta in plenty of boiling salted water according to the instructions on the packet.

2 Heat the butter in a large frying pan and fry the onion for about 10 minutes, or until softened.

3 Add the garlic, bay leaf and wine and bring to the boil. Boil rapidly until reduced by about half. Remove the bay leaf, then stir in the crème fraîche and return to the boil.

4 Add the chicken, ham and Gouda cheese and simmer for 5 minutes, stirring occasionally until heated through.

5 Add the chopped fresh mint and season to taste.

6 Drain the pasta thoroughly and turn it into a large serving dish. Toss with the sauce, garnish with finely shredded fresh mint and serve immediately.

Cheesy Pasta Bolognese

*Mozzarella gives the cheese sauce a
particularly creamy taste.*

INGREDIENTS

Serves 4

30ml/2 tbsp olive oil

1 onion, chopped

1 garlic clove, crushed

1 carrot, diced

2 celery sticks, chopped

2 rashers streaky bacon, finely chopped

5 button mushrooms, chopped

450g/1lb lean minced beef

120ml/4fl oz/½ cup red wine

15ml/1 tbsp tomato purée

200g/7oz can chopped tomatoes

fresh thyme sprig

225g/8oz dried penne

300ml/½ pint/1¼ cups milk

25g/1oz/2 tbsp butter

25g/1oz/2 tbsp flour

150g/5oz/1 cup cubed mozzarella cheese

60ml/4 tbsp grated Parmesan cheese

salt and ground black pepper

fresh basil sprigs, to garnish

1 Heat the oil in a pan and fry the onion, garlic, carrot and celery for 6 minutes, until the onions have softened.

2 Add the bacon and continue frying for 3–4 minutes. Stir in the mushrooms, fry for 2 minutes, then add the beef. Fry over a high heat until well browned all over.

3 Pour in the red wine, the tomato purée dissolved in 45ml/3 tbsp water, and the tomatoes, then add the thyme and season well. Bring to the boil, cover the pan and simmer gently for about 30 minutes.

4 Preheat the oven to 200°C/ 400°F/Gas 6. Bring a pan of water to the boil, add a little oil. Cook the pasta for 10 minutes.

5 Meanwhile, place the milk, butter and flour in a saucepan, heat gently and whisk constantly with a balloon whisk until the mixture is thickened. Stir in the cubed mozzarella cheese, 30ml/2 tbsp of the Parmesan and season lightly.

6 Drain the pasta and stir into the cheese sauce. Uncover the tomato sauce and boil rapidly for about 2 minutes to reduce.

7 Spoon the sauce into an ovenproof dish, top with the pasta mixture and sprinkle the remaining 30ml/2 tbsp Parmesan cheese evenly over the top. Bake for 25 minutes until golden. Garnish with basil and serve hot.

Fusilli with Turkey

Broccoli combines with the other ingredients to make a one-pan meal.

INGREDIENTS

Serves 4

675g/1½lb ripe, firm plum
    tomatoes, quartered
90ml/6 tbsp olive oil
5ml/1 tsp dried oregano
350g/12oz broccoli florets
1 small onion, sliced
5ml/1 tsp dried thyme
450g/1lb skinless, boneless turkey
    breast, cubed
3 garlic cloves, crushed
15ml/1 tbsp fresh lemon juice
450g/1lb fusilli
salt and ground black pepper

1 Preheat the oven to 200°C/ 400°F/Gas 6. Place the plum tomatoes in a baking dish. Add 15ml/1 tbsp of the oil, the oregano and 2.5ml/½ tsp salt and stir.

2 Bake for 30–40 minutes, until the tomatoes are just browned; do not stir.

3 Meanwhile, bring a large saucepan of salted water to the boil. Add the broccoli florets and cook until just tender, about 5 minutes. Drain and set aside. (Alternatively, steam the broccoli until tender.)

4 Heat 30ml/2 tbsp of the oil in a large non-stick frying pan.

Add the onion, thyme, turkey and 2.5ml/½ tsp salt. Cook over a high heat, stirring often, until the meat is cooked and beginning to brown, about 5–7 minutes. Add the garlic and cook for a further 1 minute, stirring frequently.

5 Remove from the heat. Stir in the lemon juice and season with ground black pepper. Set aside and keep warm.

6 Cook the fusilli in plenty of boiling salted water according to the instructions on the packet until *al dente*. Drain and place in a large bowl. Toss the pasta with the remaining oil.

7 Add the broccoli to the turkey mixture, then stir into the fusilli. Add the tomatoes and stir gently to blend. Serve immediately.

CHEESE &
CREAM
SAUCES

~

Tagliatelle with Gorgonzola Sauce

Gorgonzola is a creamy Italian blue cheese. As an alternative you could use Danish Blue or Pipo Creme.

INGREDIENTS

Serves 4

25g/1oz/2 tbsp butter, plus extra for
    tossing the pasta
225g/8oz Gorgonzola cheese
150ml/¼ pint/⅔ cup double or
    whipping cream
30ml/2 tbsp dry vermouth
5ml/1 tsp cornflour
15ml/1 tbsp chopped fresh sage
450g/1lb tagliatelle
salt and ground black pepper

1 Melt 25g/1oz/2 tbsp butter in a heavy saucepan (it needs to be thick-based to prevent the cheese from burning). Stir in 175g/6oz crumbled Gorgonzola cheese and stir over a gentle heat for about 2–3 minutes until melted.

2 Whisk in the cream, vermouth and cornflour. Add the sage; season. Cook, whisking, until the sauce boils and thickens. Set aside.

3 Boil the pasta in plenty of salted water according to the instructions on the packet. Drain well and toss with a little butter.

4 Reheat the sauce gently, whisking well. Divide the pasta among four serving bowls, top with the sauce and sprinkle over the remaining crumbled cheese. Serve immediately.

Ravioli with Four-cheese Sauce

This is a smooth, cheesy sauce that coats the pasta very evenly.

INGREDIENTS

Serves 4

350g/12oz ravioli

50g/2oz/¼ cup butter

50g/2oz/¼ cup plain flour

450ml/¾ pint/1¾ cups milk

50g/2oz Parmesan cheese

50g/2oz Edam cheese

50g/2oz Gruyère cheese

50g/2oz fontina cheese

salt and ground black pepper

chopped fresh flat leaf parsley, to garnish

1 Cook the pasta in plenty of boiling salted water according to the instructions on the packet.

2 Melt the butter in a saucepan, stir in the flour and cook for 2 minutes, stirring occasionally.

3 Gradually stir in the milk until completely blended.

4 Bring the milk slowly to the boil, stirring constantly until the sauce is thickened.

5 Grate the cheeses and stir them into the sauce. Stir until they are just beginning to melt. Remove from the heat and season.

6 Drain the pasta thoroughly and turn into a large serving dish. Pour over the sauce and toss to coat. Serve immediately, garnished with the chopped fresh parsley.

Tortellini with Cream, Butter and Cheese

This is an indulgent but quick alternative to macaroni cheese. Stir in some ham or pepperoni if you wish, though it's quite delicious as it is!

INGREDIENTS

Serves 4–6

450g/1lb fresh tortellini

50g/2oz/4 tbsp butter

300ml/½ pint/1¼ cups double cream

115g/4oz Parmesan cheese

freshly grated nutmeg

salt and ground black pepper

3 Grate the Parmesan cheese and stir 75g/3oz/¾ cup of it into the sauce until melted. Season to taste with salt, black pepper and nutmeg. Preheat the grill.

4 Drain the pasta well and spoon into a buttered heatproof serving dish. Pour over the sauce, sprinkle over the remaining cheese and place under the grill until brown and bubbling. Serve the tortellini immediately.

1 Cook the pasta in plenty of boiling salted water according to the instructions on the packet.

2 Meanwhile melt the butter in a medium saucepan and stir in the cream. Bring to the boil and cook for 2–3 minutes until the mixture is slightly thickened.

Macaroni Cheese with Mushrooms

Macaroni cheese is an all-time classic from the mid-week menu. Here it is served in a light creamy sauce with mushrooms and topped with pine nuts.

INGREDIENTS

Serves 4

450g/1lb quick-cooking elbow macaroni
45ml/3 tbsp olive oil
225g/8oz button mushrooms, sliced
2 fresh thyme sprigs
60ml/4 tbsp plain flour
1 vegetable stock cube
600ml/1 pint/2½ cups milk
2.5ml/½ tsp celery salt
5ml/1 tsp Dijon mustard
175g/6oz/1½ cups grated
    Cheddar cheese
25g/1oz/¼ cup freshly grated
    Parmesan cheese
25g/1oz/2 tbsp pine nuts
salt and ground black pepper

1 Cook the macaroni in plenty of boiling salted water according to the instructions on the packet.

COOK'S TIP

Closed button mushrooms are best for white cream sauces. Open varieties can darken a pale sauce to an unattractive sludgy grey.

2 Heat the oil in a heavy-based saucepan. Add the mushrooms and thyme, cover and cook over a gentle heat for 2–3 minutes. Stir in the flour and remove from the heat, add the stock cube and stir continuously until evenly blended. Add the milk, a little at a time, stirring after each addition. Add the celery salt, mustard and Cheddar cheese and season. Stir and simmer for 1–2 minutes until the sauce is thickened.

3 Preheat a moderate grill. Drain the macaroni; toss into the sauce. Turn into four individual dishes or one large flameproof gratin dish. Scatter with grated Parmesan cheese and pine nuts; grill until brown and bubbly.

Pasta with Tomato and Cream Sauce

Here pasta is served with a deliciously rich version of an ordinary tomato sauce.

INGREDIENTS

Serves 4–6

30ml/2 tbsp olive oil

2 garlic cloves, crushed

400g/14oz can chopped tomatoes

150ml/¼ pint/⅔ cup double or whipping cream

30ml/2 tbsp chopped fresh herbs, such as basil, oregano or parsley

450g/1lb pasta, any variety

salt and ground black pepper

1 Heat the oil in a medium saucepan, add the garlic and cook for 2 minutes, until golden.

2 Stir in the tomatoes, bring to the boil and simmer uncovered for 20 minutes, stirring occasionally to prevent sticking. The sauce is ready when you can see the oil separating on top.

3 Add the cream, bring slowly to the boil again and simmer until slightly thickened. Stir in the herbs, taste and season well.

4 Cook the pasta in plenty of boiling salted water according to the instructions on the packet. Drain well and toss with the sauce. Serve piping hot, sprinkled with extra herbs, if you like.

Pasta Twists with Cream and Cheese

Soured cream and two cheeses make a lovely rich sauce.

INGREDIENTS

Serves 4

350g/12oz pasta twists, such as spirali

25g/1oz/2 tbsp butter

1 onion, chopped

1 garlic clove, chopped

15ml/1 tbsp chopped fresh oregano

300ml/½ pint/1¼ cups soured cream

75g/3oz/¾ cup grated mozzarella cheese

75g/3oz/¾ cup grated Bel Paese cheese

5 sun-dried tomatoes in oil, drained
   and sliced

salt and ground black pepper

1 Cook the pasta in plenty of boiling salted water according to the instructions on the packet.

2 Melt the butter in a large frying pan and fry the onion for about 10 minutes until softened. Add the garlic and cook for 1 minute.

3 Stir in the oregano and cream and heat gently until almost boiling. Stir in the mozzarella and Bel Paese cheese and heat gently, stirring occasionally, until melted. Add the sun-dried tomatoes and season to taste.

4 Drain the pasta twists well and turn into a serving dish. Pour over the sauce and toss well to coat. Serve immediately.

Canneroni with Cheese and Coriander

A speedy supper dish, this is best served with a simple tomato and fresh basil salad.

INGREDIENTS

Serves 4

450g/1lb canneroni

115g/4oz full-fat garlic-and-herb cheese

30ml/2 tbsp very finely chopped
   fresh coriander

300ml/½ pint/1¼ cups single cream

115g/4oz/1 cup shelled peas, cooked

salt and ground black pepper

1 Cook the pasta in plenty of boiling salted water according to the instructions on the packet.

2 Melt the cheese in a small pan over a low heat until smooth.

3 Stir in the coriander, cream and salt and pepper. Bring slowly to the boil, stirring occasionally, until well blended. Stir in the peas and continue cooking until heated through.

4 Drain the pasta and turn into a large serving dish. Pour over the sauce and toss well to coat thoroughly. Serve immediately.

COOK'S TIP

If you do not like the pronounced flavour of fresh coriander, substitute another fresh herb, such as basil or flat leaf parsley.

Curly Spaghetti with Walnuts and Cream

A classic Italian dish with a strong, nutty flavour, this should be served with a delicately flavoured salad.

INGREDIENTS

Serves 4

350g/12oz curly spaghetti (fusilli col buco)

50g/2oz/½ cup walnut pieces

25g/1oz/2 tbsp butter

300ml/½ pint/1¼ cups milk

50g/2oz/1 cup fresh breadcrumbs

25g/1oz/2 tbsp freshly grated Parmesan cheese

pinch of freshly grated nutmeg

salt and ground black pepper

fresh rosemary sprigs, to garnish

1 Cook the pasta in plenty of boiling salted water according to the instructions on the packet. Meanwhile, preheat the grill.

2 Spread the walnuts evenly over the grill pan. Grill for about 5 minutes, turning occasionally until evenly toasted.

3 Remove the walnuts from the heat, place in a clean dish towel and rub away the skins. Roughly chop the nuts.

4 Heat the butter and milk in a saucepan until the butter is completely melted.

5 Stir in the breadcrumbs and nuts and heat gently for 2 minutes, stirring constantly until thickened.

6 Add the Parmesan cheese, nutmeg and seasoning to taste.

7 Drain the pasta thoroughly through a colander and toss in the sauce. Serve immediately, garnished with fresh sprigs of rosemary.

Spaghetti with Feta Cheese

We think of pasta as being essentially Italian but, in fact, the Greeks have a great appetite for it too. It complements tangy, full-flavoured feta cheese beautifully in this simple but effective dish.

INGREDIENTS

Serves 2–3

115g/4oz spaghetti

1 garlic clove

30ml/2 tbsp extra virgin olive oil

8 cherry tomatoes, halved

a little freshly grated nutmeg

salt and ground black pepper

75g/3oz feta cheese, crumbled

15ml/1 tbsp chopped fresh basil

a few black olives, to serve (optional)

1 Cook the spaghetti in plenty of boiling salted water according to the instructions on the packet, then drain well.

2 In the same pan gently heat the garlic clove in the olive oil for 1–2 minutes, then add the halved cherry tomatoes.

3 Increase the heat to fry the tomatoes lightly for 1 minute, then remove the garlic and discard.

4 Toss in the spaghetti, season with the nutmeg and salt and pepper to taste, then stir in the crumbled feta cheese and basil.

5 Check the seasoning, remembering that feta can be quite salty, and serve hot topped with black olives, if desired.

FISH &
SHELLFISH
SAUCES

~

Spaghetti with Mixed Shellfish Sauce

A special occasion sauce for an evening of entertaining is just what this is, so serve it in bountiful portions to your guests.

INGREDIENTS

Serves 4

50g/2oz/4 tbsp butter

2 shallots, chopped

2 garlic cloves, chopped

350g/12oz spaghetti

2 tbsp finely chopped fresh basil

300ml/½ pint/1¼ cups dry white wine

450g/1lb mussels, scrubbed

115g/4oz squid, washed

5ml/1 tsp chilli powder

350g/12oz raw peeled prawns

300ml/½ pint/1¼ cups soured cream

salt and ground black pepper

50g/2oz/⅓ cup Parmesan cheese,
   freshly grated

chopped fresh flat leaf parsley, to garnish

to the pan, cover and simmer for about 5 minutes until all the shells have opened. Discard any mussels that do not open. Using a slotted spoon, transfer the mussels to a plate, remove them from their shells and return to the pan. Reserve a few mussels in the shells for garnishing.

5 Meanwhile, slice the squid into thin circles. Melt the remaining butter in a frying pan and fry the remaining shallot and garlic for about 5 minutes until softened.

6 Add the remaining basil, the squid, chilli powder and prawns to the pan and stir-fry for 5 minutes until the prawns have turned pink and tender.

7 Turn the mussel mixture into the prawn mixture and bring to the boil. Stir in the soured cream and season to taste. Bring almost to the boil and simmer for 1 minute.

8 Drain the pasta thoroughly and stir it into the sauce with the Parmesan cheese until well coated. Serve immediately, garnished with chopped flat leaf parsley and the reserved mussels in their shells.

1 Melt half the butter in a frying pan and fry 1 shallot and 1 garlic clove for about 5 minutes until softened.

2 Cook the pasta in plenty of boiling salted water according to the instructions on the packet.

3 Stir in half the basil and the wine and bring to the boil.

4 Discard any mussels that are open and do not shut when tapped with the back of a knife. Quickly add the remaining mussels

Spaghetti with Mussels

Mussels are popular in all the coastal regions of Italy, and are delicious with pasta. This simple dish is greatly improved by using the freshest mussels available.

INGREDIENTS

Serves 4

900g/2lb fresh mussels, in the shell

75ml/5 tbsp olive oil

3 garlic cloves, finely chopped

60ml/4 tbsp chopped fresh parsley

60ml/4 tbsp white wine

400g/14oz spaghetti

salt and ground black pepper

2 Place the mussels with a cupful of water in a large saucepan over a moderate heat. As soon as they open, lift them out one by one with a slotted spoon.

1 Scrub the mussels well under cold running water, carefully cutting off the "beards" with a small sharp knife. Discard any that do not close when tapped sharply.

3 When all the mussels have opened (discard any that do not), strain the liquid in the saucepan through a layer of kitchen paper to remove any grit, and reserve until needed.

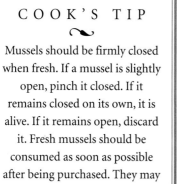

COOK'S TIP

Mussels should be firmly closed when fresh. If a mussel is slightly open, pinch it closed. If it remains closed on its own, it is alive. If it remains open, discard it. Fresh mussels should be consumed as soon as possible after being purchased. They may be kept in a bowl of cold water in the fridge.

4 Heat the oil in a large frying pan. Add the garlic and parsley, and cook for 2–3 minutes. Add the mussels, their cooking liquid and the wine. Cook over a moderate heat until heated through.

5 Add a generous amount of pepper to the sauce. Taste for seasoning; add salt if necessary.

6 Cook the pasta in plenty of boiling salted water until *al dente*. Drain, then tip it into the frying pan with the sauce, and stir well over a moderate heat for 3–4 minutes. Serve at once.

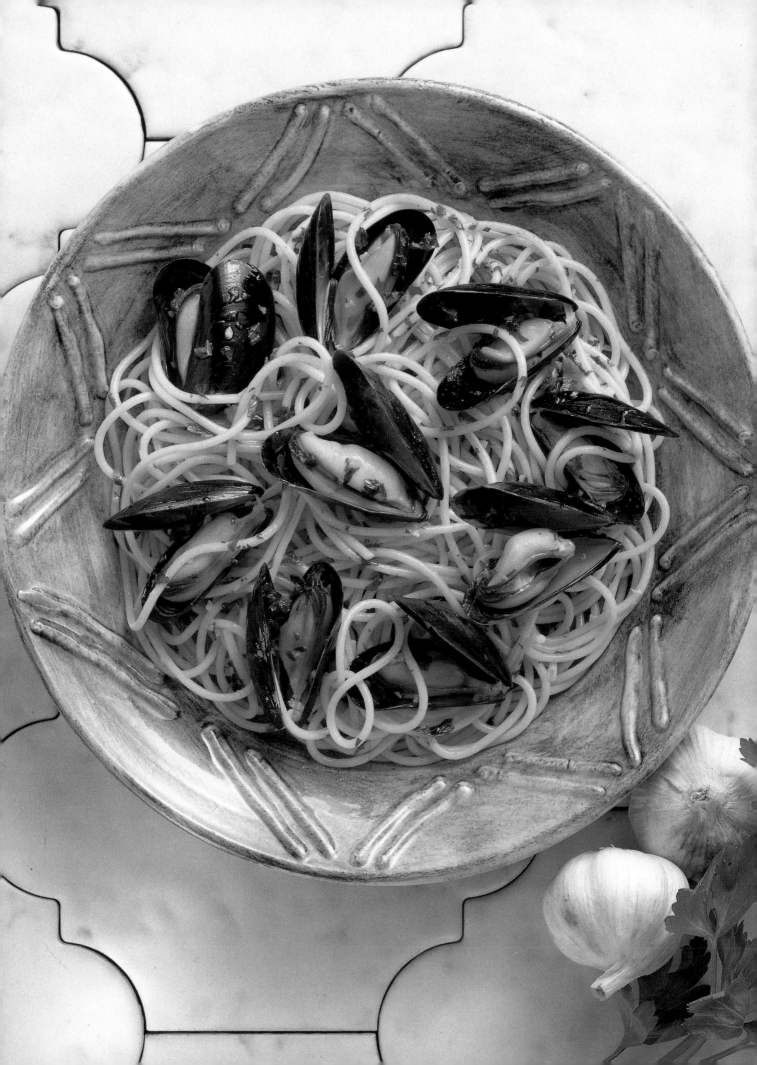

Linguine with Clams, Leeks and Tomatoes

Canned clams make this a speedy dish for those in a real hurry.

INGREDIENTS

Serves 4

350g/12oz linguine

25g/1oz/2 tbsp butter

2 leeks, thinly sliced

150ml/¼ pint/⅔ cup dry white wine

4 tomatoes, skinned, seeded and chopped

pinch of turmeric (optional)

250g/9oz can clams, drained

30ml/2 tbsp chopped fresh basil

60ml/4 tbsp crème fraîche

salt and ground black pepper

1 Cook the pasta in plenty of boiling salted water according to the instructions on the packet.

2 Meanwhile, melt the butter in a small saucepan and fry the sliced leeks for about 5 minutes until softened.

3 Add the wine, tomatoes and turmeric, bring to the boil and boil until reduced by half.

4 Stir in the clams, basil, crème fraîche and seasoning and heat through gently without boiling the sauce.

5 Drain the pasta thoroughly and toss in the clam and leek sauce. Serve immediately.

Macaroni with King Prawns and Ham

Cooked radicchio makes a novel addition to this sauce.

INGREDIENTS

Serves 4

350g/12oz short macaroni

45ml/3 tbsp olive oil

12 shelled raw king prawns

1 garlic clove, chopped

175g/6oz/generous 1 cup diced
   smoked ham

150ml/¼ pint/⅔ cup red wine

½ small radicchio lettuce, shredded

2 egg yolks, beaten

30ml/2 tbsp chopped fresh flat leaf parsley

150ml/¼ pint/⅔ cup double cream

salt and ground black pepper

shredded fresh basil, to garnish

1 Cook the pasta in plenty of boiling salted water, according to the instructions on the packet.

2 Meanwhile, heat the oil in a frying pan and cook the prawns, garlic and ham for about 5 minutes, stirring occasionally until the prawns are tender. Be careful not to overcook.

3 Add the wine and radicchio, bring to the boil and boil rapidly until the juices are reduced by about half.

4 Stir in the egg yolks, parsley and cream and bring almost to the boil, stirring constantly, then simmer until the sauce thickens slightly. Check the seasoning and adjust if necessary.

5 Drain the pasta thoroughly and toss in the sauce to coat. Serve immediately, garnished with some shredded fresh basil.

Spaghetti with Tomato and Clam Sauce

Small sweet clams make this a delicately succulent sauce. Cockles would make a good substitute, or even mussels, but don't be tempted to use seafood pickled in vinegar.

INGREDIENTS

Serves 4

900g/2lb live small clams in the shell,
   or 2 x 400g/14oz cans clams in
   brine, drained
90ml/6 tbsp olive oil
2 garlic cloves, crushed
500g/1¼lb canned chopped tomatoes
45ml/3 tbsp chopped fresh parsley
450g/1lb spaghetti
salt and ground black pepper

1 If using live clams, place them in a bowl of cold water and rinse several times to remove any grit or sand, then drain well.

2 Heat the oil in a saucepan and add the clams. Stir over a high heat until the clams open. Discard any that do not open. Transfer the clams to a bowl with a slotted spoon and set aside.

3 Reduce the clam juice left in the pan to almost nothing by boiling fast. Add the garlic and fry until golden. Pour in the tomatoes, bring to the boil and cook for 3–4 minutes until reduced. Stir in the clam mixture or canned clams and half the parsley and heat through. Season to taste.

4 Cook the pasta in plenty of boiling salted water according to the instructions on the packet. Drain well and turn into a warm serving dish. Pour over the sauce and sprinkle with the remaining chopped parsley.

Tagliatelle with Haddock and Avocado

You will need to start this recipe the day before because the haddock should be left to marinate overnight.

INGREDIENTS

Serves 4

350g/12oz fresh haddock fillets, skinned

2.5ml/½ tsp each ground cumin, ground
    coriander and turmeric

150ml/¼ pint/⅔ cup fromage frais

150ml/¼ pint/⅔ cup double cream

15ml/1 tbsp lemon juice

25g/1oz/2 tbsp butter

1 onion, chopped

15ml/1 tbsp plain flour

150ml/¼ pint/⅔ cup fish stock

350g/12oz tagliatelle

1 avocado, peeled, stoned and sliced

2 tomatoes, seeded and chopped

salt and ground black pepper

fresh rosemary sprigs, to garnish

1 Carefully cut the haddock into bite-size pieces.

2 Mix together all the spices, seasoning, fromage frais, cream and lemon juice.

3 Stir in the haddock to coat. Cover the dish and leave to marinate overnight.

4 Heat the butter in a frying pan and fry the onion for about 10 minutes until softened. Stir in the flour, then blend in the stock until smooth.

5 Carefully stir in the haddock mixture until well blended. Bring to the boil, stirring, cover and simmer for about 30 seconds. Remove from the heat.

6 Meanwhile, cook the pasta in plenty of boiling salted water according to the instructions on the packet.

7 Stir the avocado and tomatoes into the haddock mixture.

8 Drain the pasta thoroughly and divide among four serving plates. Spoon over the sauce and serve immediately, garnished with fresh rosemary.

Salmon Pasta with Parsley Sauce

This dish is so quick and easy to make – and delicious.

INGREDIENTS

Serves 4

450g/1lb salmon fillet, skinned
225g/8oz pasta, such as penne or twists
175g/6oz cherry tomatoes, halved
150ml/¼ pint/⅔ cup low -fat crème fraîche
45ml/3 tbsp finely chopped parsley
finely grated rind of ½ orange
salt and ground black pepper

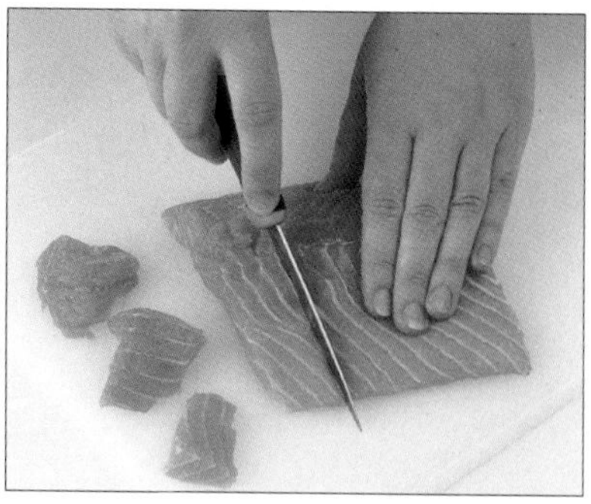

1 Cut the salmon into bite-size pieces, arrange on a heatproof plate and cover with foil.

2 Bring a large pan of salted water to the boil, add the pasta and return to the boil. Place the plate of salmon on top and simmer for 10–12 minutes, until the pasta and salmon are cooked.

3 Drain the pasta and toss with the tomatoes and salmon. Mix together the crème fraîche, parsley, orange rind and pepper to taste, then toss into the salmon and pasta and serve hot or cold.

Pasta with Scallops and Tomato Sauce

Fresh basil gives this sauce a distinctive flavour.

INGREDIENTS

Serves 4

450g/1lb pasta, such as fettucine
   or linguine
30ml/2 tbsp olive oil
2 garlic cloves, crushed
450g/1lb sea scallops, halved horizontally
salt and ground black pepper
30ml/2 tbsp chopped fresh basil

For the sauce
30ml/2 tbsp olive oil
½ onion, minced
1 garlic clove, crushed
2.5ml/½ tsp salt
2 x 400g/14oz cans plum tomatoes

1 For the sauce, heat the oil in a non-stick frying pan. Add the onion, garlic and a little salt, and cook over a medium heat for about 5 minutes until just softened, stirring occasionally.

2 Add the tomatoes, with their juice, and crush with a fork. Bring to the boil, then reduce the heat and simmer gently for 15 minutes. Remove from the heat and set aside.

3 Cook the pasta in plenty of boiling salted water, according to the instructions on the packet, until *al dente*.

4 Meanwhile, combine the oil and garlic in another non-stick frying pan and cook until just sizzling, about 30 seconds. Add the scallops and 2.5ml/½ tsp salt and cook over a high heat, tossing until the scallops are cooked through, about 3 minutes.

5 Add the scallops to the tomato sauce. Season with salt and pepper, stir and keep warm.

6 Drain the pasta, rinse under hot water and drain again. Place in a large serving dish. Add the sauce and the basil and toss thoroughly. Serve immediately.

Pasta Tubes with Tuna and Olive Sauce

This colourful sauce combines well with a thicker and shorter pasta.

INGREDIENTS

Serves 4

350g/12oz rigatoni
30ml/2 tbsp olive oil
1 onion, chopped
2 garlic cloves, chopped
400g/14oz can chopped tomatoes
50g/2oz/4 tbsp tomato purée
50g/2oz/½ cup stoned black
    olives, quartered
15ml/1 tbsp chopped fresh oregano
225g/8oz can tuna in oil, drained
    and flaked
2.5ml/½ tsp anchovy purée
15ml/1 tbsp capers, rinsed
115g/4oz/1 cup grated Cheddar cheese
45ml/3 tbsp fresh white breadcrumbs
salt and ground black pepper
flat leaf parsley sprigs, to garnish

1 Cook the pasta in plenty of boiling salted water according to the instructions on the packet.

2 Meanwhile, heat the oil in a frying pan and fry the onion and garlic for about 10 minutes until softened.

3 Add the tomatoes, tomato purée, and salt and pepper, and bring to the boil. Simmer gently for 5 minutes, stirring occasionally.

4 Stir in the olives, oregano, tuna, anchovy purée and capers. Spoon the mixture into a mixing bowl.

5 Drain the pasta, toss well in the sauce and spoon into flame-proof serving dishes.

6 Preheat the grill and sprinkle the cheese and breadcrumbs over the pasta. Grill for about 10 minutes until the pasta is heated through and the cheese has melted. Serve at once, garnished with flat leaf parsley.

Tagliatelle with Saffron Mussels

Mussels in a saffron and cream sauce are served with tagliatelle in this recipe, but you can use any other pasta if you prefer.

INGREDIENTS

Serves 4

1.75kg/4–4½lb live mussels in the shell

150ml/¼ pint/⅔ cup dry white wine

2 shallots, chopped

350g/12oz dried tagliatelle

25g/1oz/2 tbsp butter

2 garlic cloves, crushed

250ml/8fl oz/1 cup double cream

generous pinch of saffron strands

1 egg yolk

salt and ground black pepper

30ml/2 tbsp chopped fresh parsley, to garnish

1 Scrub the mussels well under cold running water. Remove the "beards" and discard any mussels that are open.

2 Place the mussels in a large pan with the wine and shallots. Cover and cook over a high heat, shaking the pan occasionally, for 5-8 minutes until the mussels have opened. Drain the mussels, reserving the liquid. Discard any that remain closed. Shell all but a few of the mussels and keep warm.

3 Bring the reserved cooking liquid to the boil, then reduce by half. Strain into a jug to remove any grit.

4 Cook the tagliatelle in plenty of boiling salted water for about 10 minutes, until *al dente*.

5 Meanwhile, melt the butter and fry the garlic for 1 minute. Pour in the mussel liquid, cream and saffron strands. Heat gently until the sauce thickens slightly. Off the heat, stir in the egg yolk, shelled mussels, and season.

6 Drain the tagliatelle and transfer to warmed serving bowls. Spoon the sauce over and sprinkle with chopped parsley. Garnish with the mussels in shells and serve at once.

Seafood Pasta Shells with Spinach Sauce

You'll need very large pasta shells, measuring about 4cm/1½in long for this dish; don't try stuffing smaller shells – they will be much too fiddly!

INGREDIENTS

Serves 4

15g/½oz/1 tbsp margarine

8 spring onions, finely sliced

6 tomatoes

32 large dried pasta shells

225g/8oz/1 cup low-fat soft cheese

90ml/6 tbsp skimmed milk

pinch of freshly grated nutmeg

225g/8oz/2 cups prawns

175g/6oz can white crab meat, drained and flaked

115g/4oz frozen chopped spinach, thawed and drained

salt and ground black pepper

1 Preheat the oven to 150°C/ 300°F/Gas 2. Melt the margarine in a small saucepan and gently cook the spring onions for 3–4 minutes, or until softened.

2 Slash the bottoms of the tomatoes, plunge into a saucepan of boiling water for 45 seconds, then into a saucepan of cold water. Slip off the skins. Halve the tomatoes, remove the seeds and cores and roughly chop the flesh.

3 Cook the pasta shells in plenty of boiling salted water for about 10 minutes, or until *al dente*. Drain well.

4 Heat the soft cheese and milk in a saucepan, stirring until blended. Season with salt, pepper and nutmeg. Measure 30ml/2 tbsp of the sauce into a bowl.

5 Add the spring onions, tomatoes, prawns, and crab meat to the bowl. Mix well. Spoon the filling into the shells and place in a single layer in a shallow ovenproof dish. Cover with foil and cook in the preheated oven for 10 minutes.

6 Stir the spinach into the remaining sauce. Bring to the boil and simmer gently for 1 minute, stirring all the time. Drizzle over the pasta shells and serve hot.

Spaghetti with Seafood Sauce

The Italian name for this tomato-based sauce is marinara.

Serves 4

45ml/3 tbsp olive oil

1 onion, chopped

1 garlic clove, finely chopped

225g/8oz spaghetti

600ml/1 pint/2½ cups passata

15ml/1 tbsp tomato purée

5ml/1 tsp dried oregano

1 bay leaf

5ml/1 tsp sugar

115g/4oz/1 cup cooked peeled shrimps
  (rinsed well if canned)

115g/4oz/1 cup cooked peeled prawns

175g/6oz/1½ cups cooked clam or cockle
  meat (rinsed well if canned or bottled)

15ml/1 tbsp lemon juice

45ml/3 tbsp chopped fresh parsley

25g/1oz/2 tbsp butter

salt and ground black pepper

4 whole cooked prawns, to garnish

1 Heat the oil in a pan and add the onion and garlic. Fry over a moderate heat for 6–7 minutes, until the onions have softened.

2 Meanwhile, cook the spaghetti in a large saucepan of boiling salted water for 10–12 minutes until *al dente*.

3 Stir the passata, tomato purée, oregano, bay leaf and sugar into the onions and season well. Bring to the boil, then simmer for 2–3 minutes.

4 Add the shellfish, lemon juice and 30ml/2 tbsp of the parsley. Stir well, then cover and cook for 6–7 minutes.

5 Meanwhile, drain the spaghetti when it is ready and add the butter to the pan. Return the drained spaghetti to the pan and toss in the butter. Season well.

6 Divide the spaghetti among four warmed plates and top with the seafood sauce. Sprinkle with the remaining chopped parsley, garnish with whole prawns and serve immediately.

Pasta with Fresh Sardine Sauce

In this classic Sicilian dish, fresh sardines are combined with raisins and pine nuts.

INGREDIENTS

Serves 4

30g/1¼oz/3 tbsp sultanas

450g/1lb fresh sardines

90ml/6 tbsp breadcrumbs

1 small fennel bulb

90ml/6 tbsp olive oil

1 onion, very thinly sliced

30g/1¼oz/3 tbsp pine nuts

2.5ml/½ tsp fennel seeds

400g/14oz long hollow pasta, such as
   percatelli, zite or bucatini

salt and ground black pepper

1 Soak the sultanas in warm water for 15 minutes. Drain and pat dry.

2 Clean the sardines. Open each one out flat and remove the central bones and head. Wash well and shake dry. Sprinkle evenly with the breadcrumbs.

3 Coarsely chop the top fronds of fennel and reserve. Pull off a few outer leaves and wash. Fill a large saucepan with enough water to cook the pasta. Add the fennel leaves and bring to the boil.

4 Heat the oil in a large frying pan and sauté the onion lightly until soft. Remove to a side dish. Add the sardines, a few at a time, and cook over a moderate heat until golden on both sides, turning once. When all the sardines have been cooked, gently return them to the pan. Add the onion, and the sultanas, pine nuts and fennel seeds. Season with salt and pepper.

5 Take about 60ml/4 tbsp of the boiling water for the pasta, and add it to the sauce. Add salt to the boiling water, and cook the pasta until *al dente*. Drain, and remove the fennel leaves. Dress the pasta with the sauce. Divide among four individual serving plates, arranging several sardines on each. Sprinkle with the reserved chopped fennel tops and serve at once.

Pasta with Spinach and Anchovy Sauce

Deliciously earthy, this would make a good starter or light supper dish. Add some sultanas to the sauce to ring the changes.

INGREDIENTS

Serves 4

900g/2lb fresh spinach or 500g/1¼lb
    frozen leaf spinach, thawed

450g/1lb angel hair pasta

salt, to taste

60ml/4 tbsp olive oil

45ml/3 tbsp pine nuts

2 garlic cloves

6 canned anchovy fillets, drained and
    chopped, or whole salted anchovies,
    rinsed, boned and chopped

butter, for tossing the pasta

1 If using fresh spinach, wash it well and remove any tough stalks. Drain thoroughly. Place in a large saucepan with only the water that clings to the leaves. Cover with a lid and cook over a high heat, shaking the pan occasionally, until the spinach is just wilted and still bright green. Drain.

2 Cook the pasta in plenty of boiling salted water according to the instructions on the packet.

3 Heat the oil in a saucepan and fry the pine nuts until golden. Remove with a slotted spoon. Add the garlic to the oil in the pan and fry until golden. Add the chopped anchovies to the pan.

4 Stir in the spinach and cook for 2–3 minutes or until heated through. Stir in the pine nuts. Drain the pasta, toss in a little butter and turn into a warmed serving dish. Top with the hot sauce and fork through roughly before serving.

Rigatoni with Scallop Sauce

*A jewel from the sea, the scallop is
what makes this sauce so special.
Serve with a green salad, if liked.*

INGREDIENTS

Serves 4

350g/12oz rigatoni

350g/12oz queen scallops

45ml/3 tbsp olive oil

1 garlic clove, chopped

1 onion, chopped

2 carrots, cut into matchsticks

30 ml/2 tbsp chopped fresh parsley

30ml/2 tbsp dry white wine

30ml/2 tbsp Pernod

150ml/¼ pint/⅔ cup double cream

salt and ground black pepper

1 Cook the pasta in plenty of
boiling salted water according
to the instructions on the packet.

2 Trim the scallops, separating
the corals from the white eye
part of the meat.

3 Using a sharp knife, cut the eye
in half lengthways.

4 Heat the oil in a frying pan
and fry the garlic, onion and
carrots for 5–10 minutes until the
carrots are softened.

5 Stir in the scallops, parsley,
wine and Pernod and bring to
the boil. Cover and simmer for
about 1 minute. Using a slotted
spoon, transfer the scallops and
vegetables to a plate and keep them
warm until required.

6 Bring the pan juices back to
the boil and boil rapidly until
reduced by half. Stir in the cream
and heat the sauce through.

7 Return the scallops and vegetables to the pan and heat them
through. Season to taste.

8 Drain the pasta thoroughly
and toss with the sauce. Serve
the rigatoni immediately.

Fusilli with Vegetable and Prawn Sauce

You will need to start this recipe the day before because the prawns should be left to marinate overnight.

Serves 4

450g/1lb/4 cups cooked peeled prawns

60ml/4 tbsp soy sauce

45ml/3 tbsp olive oil

350g/12oz curly spaghetti (fusilli col buco)

1 yellow pepper, cored, seeded and cut into strips

225g/8oz broccoli florets

1 bunch spring onions, shredded

2.5cm/1in piece fresh ginger root, peeled and shredded

15ml/1 tbsp chopped fresh oregano

30ml/2 tbsp dry sherry

15ml/1 tbsp cornflour

300ml/½ pint/1¼ cups fish stock

salt and ground black pepper

1 Place the prawns in a mixing bowl. Stir in half the soy sauce and 30ml/2 tbsp of the olive oil. Cover and marinate overnight.

2 Cook the pasta in plenty of boiling salted water according to the instructions on the packet.

3 Meanwhile, heat the remaining oil in a wok or frying pan and fry the prawns for 1 minute.

4 Add the pepper, broccoli, spring onions, ginger and oregano and stir-fry for about 1–2 minutes.

5 Drain the pasta thoroughly, set aside and keep warm. Meanwhile, blend together the sherry and cornflour until smooth. Stir in the stock and remaining soy sauce until well blended.

6 Pour the sauce into the wok or pan, bring to the boil and stir-fry for 2 minutes until thickened. Pour over the pasta and serve.

Mixed Summer Pasta

A pretty and colourful sauce with bags of flavour makes this a popular dish for the summer.

Serves 4

115g/4oz French beans, cut into
   2.5cm/1in pieces
350g/12oz curly spaghetti (fusilli
   col buco)
30ml/2 tbsp olive oil
½ fennel bulb, sliced
1 bunch spring onions, sliced diagonally
115g/4oz yellow cherry tomatoes
115g/4oz red cherry tomatoes
30ml/2 tbsp chopped fresh dill
225g/8oz/2 cups cooked peeled prawns
15ml/1 tbsp lemon juice
15ml/1 tbsp wholegrain mustard
60ml/4 tbsp soured cream
salt and ground black pepper
fresh dill sprigs, to garnish

1 Cook the beans in a saucepan of boiling salted water for about 5 minutes until tender. Drain through a colander.

2 Cook the pasta in plenty of boiling salted water, according to the instructions on the packet, until *al dente*.

3 Heat the oil in a frying pan and fry the sliced fennel and spring onions for about 5 minutes.

4 Stir in all the cherry tomatoes and fry for a further 5 minutes, stirring occasionally.

5 Add the dill and prawns and cook for 1 minute.

6 Stir in the lemon juice, wholegrain mustard, soured cream, seasoning and beans and simmer for 1 minute.

7 Drain the pasta and toss with the sauce. Serve immediately, garnished with fresh dill.

VEGETABLE
SAUCES

~

Pasta Napoletana

The simple classic cooked tomato sauce with no adornments.

Serves 4

900g/2lb fresh ripe red tomatoes or 750g/1¾lb canned plum tomatoes with their juice

1 onion, chopped

1 carrot, diced

1 celery stick, diced

150ml/¼ pint/⅔ cup dry white wine (optional)

1 sprig fresh parsley

pinch of caster sugar

15ml/1 tbsp chopped fresh oregano or 5ml/1 tsp dried

450g/1lb pasta, any variety

salt and ground black pepper

freshly grated Parmesan cheese, to serve

1 Roughly chop the tomatoes and place in a medium saucepan.

2 Add all the other ingredients, except the oregano, pasta and cheese, and bring to the boil. Simmer, half-covered, for about 45 minutes until very thick, stirring occasionally. Strain, then stir in the oregano. Taste and adjust the seasoning if necessary.

3 Cook the pasta in plenty of boiling salted water according to the instructions on the packet, until *al dente*. Drain well.

4 Toss the pasta with the sauce. Serve with plenty of freshly grated Parmesan cheese.

Spaghetti with Herb Sauce

Herbs make a wonderfully aromatic sauce – the heat from the pasta releases their flavours.

INGREDIENTS

Serves 4

50g/2oz chopped fresh mixed herbs, such as parsley, basil and thyme

2 garlic cloves, crushed

60ml/4 tbsp pine nuts, toasted

150ml/¼ pint/⅔ cup olive oil

350g/12oz dried spaghetti

60ml/4 tbsp freshly grated Parmesan cheese

salt and ground black pepper

basil leaves, to garnish

1 Put the herbs, garlic and half the pine nuts into a blender or food processor. With the machine running slowly, add the oil and process to form a thick purée.

2 Cook the spaghetti in plenty of boiling salted water for about 8 minutes until *al dente*. Drain.

3 Transfer the herb purée to a large warmed serving dish, then add the spaghetti and Parmesan. Toss well to coat the pasta with the sauce. Sprinkle over the remaining pine nuts and the basil leaves and serve immediately.

Pasta with Courgette and Walnut Sauce

The vegetables are softened slowly to release their flavours.

INGREDIENTS

Serves 4

65g/2½oz/5 tbsp butter

1 large Spanish onion, halved and
   thinly sliced

450g/1lb courgettes, very thinly sliced

375g/12oz short pasta shapes, such as
   penne, ziti, rotini or fusilli

50g/2oz/½ cup walnuts, coarsely chopped

45ml/3 tbsp chopped fresh parsley

30ml/2 tbsp single cream

salt and ground black pepper

freshly grated Parmesan cheese, to serve

1 Melt the butter in a frying pan. Add the onion, cover and sweat for 5 minutes until translucent, then add the courgettes.

2 Stir well, cover again and sweat until the vegetables are very soft, stirring occasionally.

3 Meanwhile, cook the pasta in plenty of boiling salted water, according to the instructions on the packet, until *al dente*.

4 While the pasta is cooking, add the walnuts, parsley and cream to the courgette mixture and stir well. Season with salt and pepper.

5 Drain the pasta and return to the pan. Add the courgette sauce and mix together well. Serve immediately, with freshly grated Parmesan to sprinkle over.

Tagliatelle with Sun-dried Tomatoes

Choose plain sun-dried tomatoes for this sauce, instead of those preserved in oil, if you wish to reduce the fat content of the dish.

INGREDIENTS

Serves 4

1 garlic clove, crushed

1 celery stick, finely sliced

115g/4oz/1 cup sun-dried tomatoes, finely chopped

90ml/3½fl oz/scant ½ cup red wine

8 plum tomatoes

350g/12oz dried tagliatelle

salt and ground black pepper

3 Add the plum tomatoes to the saucepan and simmer for a further 5 minutes. Season to taste.

4 Meanwhile, cook the tagliatelle in plenty of boiling salted water for 8–10 minutes, or until *al dente*. Drain well. Toss with half the sauce and serve on warmed plates, with the remaining sauce.

1 Put the garlic, celery, sun-dried tomatoes and wine into a large saucepan. Gently cook for about 15 minutes.

2 Slash the bottoms of the plum tomatoes and plunge into a saucepan of boiling water for 1 minute, then into a saucepan of cold water. Slip off their skins. Halve, remove the seeds and cores and roughly chop the flesh.

Macaroni with Hazelnut and Coriander Sauce

This is a variation on pesto sauce, giving a smooth, herby flavour of coriander.

INGREDIENTS

Serves 4

350g/12oz macaroni

50g/2oz/⅓ cup hazelnuts

2 garlic cloves

1 bunch fresh coriander

1 tsp salt

90ml/6 tbsp olive oil

fresh coriander sprigs, to garnish

1 Cook the pasta following the instructions on the packet, until *al dente*.

2 Meanwhile, finely chop the hazelnuts.

COOK'S TIP

To remove the skins from the hazelnuts, place them in a 180°C/350°F/Gas 4 oven for 20 minutes, then rub off the skins with a clean dish towel.

3 Place the nuts and remaining ingredients, except 1 tbsp of the oil, in a food processor, or use a pestle and mortar and grind together to create the sauce.

4 Heat the remaining oil in a saucepan and add the sauce. Fry very gently for about 1 minute until heated through.

5 Drain the pasta thoroughly and stir it into the sauce. Toss well to coat. Serve immediately, garnished with fresh coriander.

Spaghetti with Aubergine and Tomato

A great supper recipe – serve this aubergine and tomato dish with freshly cooked mange-touts.

Serves 4

3 small aubergines
olive oil, for frying
450g/1lb spaghetti
1 quantity Classic Tomato Sauce
    (see Curly Lasagne with Classic
    Tomato Sauce)
225g/8oz fontina cheese, grated
salt and ground black pepper

1 Top and tail the aubergines and slice thinly. Arrange in a colander, sprinkling with plenty of salt between each layer. Leave to stand for about 30 minutes.

2 Rinse the aubergines under cold running water. Drain and pat dry on kitchen paper.

3 Heat plenty of oil in a large frying pan and fry the aubergine slices in batches for about 5 minutes, turning them once during the cooking time, until evenly browned.

4 Meanwhile, cook the pasta in plenty of boiling salted water according to the instructions on the packet, until *al dente*.

5 Stir the tomato sauce into the pan with the aubergines and bring to the boil. Cover and then simmer for 5 minutes.

6 Stir in the fontina cheese and salt and pepper. Continue stirring over a medium heat until the cheese melts.

7 Drain the pasta and stir into the sauce, tossing well to coat. Serve immediately.

Pasta Spirals with Pesto Sauce

A light, fragrant sauce like this dish gives a temptingly different taste.

INGREDIENTS

Serves 4

350g/12oz pasta spirals (fusilli)

50g/2oz fresh basil leaves, without the stalks

2 garlic cloves, chopped

30ml/2 tbsp pine nuts

salt and freshly ground black pepper

150ml/¼ pint/⅔ cup olive oil

50g/2oz/⅓ cup Parmesan cheese, freshly grated, plus extra to garnish

fresh basil sprigs, to garnish

COOK'S TIP

Fresh basil is widely available from most greengrocers and supermarkets, either in growing pots or packets. If you buy a plant, remove the flowers as they appear so the plant grows more leaves.

Pesto is best kept in a screw-topped jar in the fridge for up to two days. If you want to keep it a few days longer, cover the top with a thin layer of olive oil. This can be stirred into the sauce when you are ready to add it to hot pasta.

---

1 Cook the pasta following the instructions on the packet until *al dente*.

2 To make the pesto sauce, place the basil leaves, garlic, pine nuts, seasoning and olive oil in a food processor or blender. Blend until very creamy.

3 Transfer the mixture to a bowl and stir in the freshly grated Parmesan cheese.

4 Drain the pasta thoroughly and turn it into a large bowl. Pour the sauce over and toss to coat. Divide among serving plates and serve, sprinkled with the extra Parmesan cheese and garnished with fresh basil sprigs.

Lasagne Rolls

Perhaps a more elegant presentation than ordinary lasagne, but just as tasty and popular. You will need to boil "no-need-to-cook" lasagne as it needs to be soft enough to roll!

INGREDIENTS

Serves 4

8-10 lasagne sheets
225g/8oz fresh leaf spinach, well washed
115g/4oz mushrooms, sliced
115g/4oz mozzarella cheese, thinly sliced
Lentil Bolognese (see below)

Béchamel Sauce
50g/2oz/scant ½ cup all-purpose flour
45ml/3 tbsp butter or margarine
600ml/1 pint/2½ cups milk
bay leaf
salt and ground black pepper
freshly grated nutmeg
freshly grated Parmesan or pecorino
    cheese, to serve

1 Cook the lasagne sheets according to instructions on the package, or until *al dente*. Drain and allow to cool.

2 Cook the spinach in the tiniest amount of water for 2 minutes then add the sliced mushrooms and cook for a further 2 minutes. Drain very well, pressing out all the excess liquor, and chop the spinach roughly.

3 Put all the béchamel ingredients into a saucepan and bring slowly to a boil, stirring until the sauce is thick and smooth. Simmer for 2 minutes with the bay leaf, then season well and stir in the grated nutmeg to taste.

4 Lay out the pasta sheets and spread with the béchamel sauce, spinach, mushrooms and mozzarella. Roll up each one and place in a large shallow casserole dish with the join face down in the dish.

5 Remove and discard the bay leaf and then pour the sauce over the pasta. Sprinkle the cheese and place under a hot grill to brown.

VARIATION

Needless to say, the fillings in this recipe could be any of your own choice. Another favourite is a lightly stir-fried mixture of colourful vegetables such as peppers, courgettes, aubergines and mushrooms, topped with a cheese béchamel as above, or with a fresh tomato sauce, which is especially good in summer.

Lentil Bolognese

A really useful sauce to serve with pasta, such as Lasagne Rolls (as above), as a crêpe stuffing or even as a protein-packed sauce for vegetables.

INGREDIENTS

Serves 6

1 onion
2 garlic cloves, crushed
2 carrots, coarsely grated
2 celery stalks, chopped
45ml/3 tbsp olive oil
150g/5oz/⅔ cup red lentils
14 oz can chopped tomatoes
45ml/3 tbsp tomato paste
475ml/16fl oz/2 cups stock
15ml/1 tbsp fresh marjoram, chopped, or
    5ml/1 tsp dried marjoram
salt and ground black pepper

1 In a large saucepan, gently fry the onion, garlic, carrots and celery in the oil for about 5 minutes, until they are soft.

2 Add the lentils, tomatoes, tomato paste, stock and marjoram, and season to taste.

3 Bring the mixture to a boil, then partially cover with a lid and simmer for 20 minutes until thick and soft. Use the Bolognese sauce as required.

Spaghetti with Olives and Mushrooms

A rich, pungent sauce topped with sweet cherry tomatoes.

INGREDIENTS

Serves 4

15ml/1 tbsp olive oil

1 garlic clove, chopped

225g/8oz mushrooms, chopped

150g/5oz/scant 1 cup black olives, stoned

30ml/2 tbsp chopped fresh parsley

1 red chilli, seeded and chopped

450g/1lb spaghetti

225g/8oz cherry tomatoes

Parmesan cheese shavings, to
   serve (optional)

1 Heat the oil in a large pan. Add the garlic; cook for 1 minute. Add the chopped mushrooms, cover, and cook over a medium heat for 5 minutes.

2 Place the mushrooms in a blender or food processor with the olives, parsley and red chilli. Blend until smooth.

3 Cook the pasta in plenty of boiling salted water, according to the instructions on the packet, until *al dente*. Drain well and return to the pan. Add the olive mixture and toss together until the pasta is well coated. Cover and keep warm.

4 Heat an ungreased frying pan and shake the cherry tomatoes around until they start to split, about 2–3 minutes. Serve the pasta topped with the tomatoes and garnished with Parmesan cheese shavings, if desired.

Spaghetti with Garlic and Oil

This is one of the simplest and most satisfying pasta dishes of all. It is very popular throughout Italy. Use the best quality oil available for this splendid dish.

INGREDIENTS

Serves 4

400g/14oz spaghetti

90ml/6 tbsp extra virgin olive oil

3 garlic cloves, chopped

60ml/4 tbsp chopped fresh parsley

salt and ground black pepper

freshly grated Parmesan cheese, to
    serve (optional)

1 Cook the spaghetti in plenty of boiling salted water.

2 In a large frying pan heat the oil and gently sauté the garlic until barely golden. Do not let it brown or it will taste bitter. Stir in the chopped fresh parsley, then season with salt and pepper. Remove from the heat until the pasta is ready.

3 Drain the pasta when it is barely *al dente*. Tip it into the pan with the oil and garlic, and cook together for 2–3 minutes, stirring well to coat the spaghetti with the sauce. Serve at once in a warmed serving bowl, with some Parmesan cheese, if desired.

Spaghetti with Walnut Sauce

Like pesto, this sauce is traditionally ground in a pestle and mortar, but works just as well made in a blender or food processor. It is also good on tagliatelle and other pasta noodles.

INGREDIENTS

Serves 4

115g/4oz/1 cup walnut pieces or halves

45ml/3 tbsp plain breadcrumbs

45ml/3 tbsp olive or walnut oil

45ml/3 tbsp chopped fresh parsley

1–2 garlic cloves (optional)

50g/2oz/¼ cup butter, at room
    temperature

30ml/2 tbsp double cream

400g/14oz wholemeal spaghetti

salt and ground black pepper

freshly grated Parmesan cheese, to serve

1 Drop the nuts into a small pan of boiling water, and cook for 1–2 minutes. Drain, then skin. Dry on kitchen paper. Coarsely chop and set aside about a quarter.

2 Place the remaining nuts, the breadcrumbs, oil, parsley and garlic, if using, in a blender or food processor. Process to a paste. Remove to a bowl, and stir in the softened butter and the cream. Season with salt and pepper.

3 Cook the pasta in plenty of boiling salted water, following the instructions on the packet, until *al dente*. Drain, then toss with the sauce. Sprinkle with the reserved chopped nuts, and hand round the grated Parmesan separately.

Campanelle with Yellow Pepper Sauce

Roasted yellow peppers make a deliciously sweet and creamy sauce to serve with pasta.

INGREDIENTS

Serves 4

2 yellow peppers

50g/2oz/¼ cup soft goat's cheese

115g/4oz/½ cup low-fat fromage blanc

450g/1lb short pasta, such as campanelle or fusilli

salt and ground black pepper

50g/2oz/½ cup toasted flaked almonds, to serve

1 Place the whole yellow peppers under a preheated grill until charred and blistered. Place in a plastic bag, seal and leave to cool. Then peel and remove all the seeds.

2 Place the pepper flesh in a blender or food processor with the goat's cheese and fromage blanc. Process until smooth. Season with salt and plenty of ground black pepper.

3 Cook the pasta in plenty of boiling salted water, according to the instructions on the packet, until *al dente*. Drain well.

4 Toss with the sauce and serve sprinkled with the toasted flaked almonds.

Tagliatelle with Walnut Sauce

*An unusual sauce which would
make this a spectacular dinner party
starter or satisfying supper.*

INGREDIENTS

Serves 4–6

2 thick slices wholemeal bread

300ml/½ pint/1¼ cups milk

275g/10oz/2½ cups walnut pieces

1 garlic clove, crushed

50g/2oz/½ cup freshly grated
   Parmesan cheese

90ml/6 tbsp olive oil, plus extra for
   tossing the pasta

150ml/¼ pint/⅔ cup double
   cream (optional)

450g/1lb tagliatelle

salt and ground black pepper

30ml/2 tbsp chopped fresh parsley,
   to garnish

3 Place the bread, walnuts, garlic,
Parmesan cheese and olive oil
in a blender or food processor and
blend until smooth. Season to taste
with salt and pepper. Stir in the
cream, if using.

4 Cook the pasta in plenty of
boiling salted water according
to the instructions on the packet,
drain and toss with a little olive oil.
Divide the pasta equally among
four or six bowls and place a
dollop of sauce on each portion.
Sprinkle with parsley.

1 Cut the crusts off the bread
and soak in the milk until all of
the milk is absorbed.

2 Preheat the oven to 190°C/
375°F/Gas 5. Spread the
walnuts on a baking sheet and
toast in the oven for 5 minutes.
Leave to cool.

Basic Tomato Sauce

Tomato sauce is without doubt the most popular dressing for pasta in Italy. This sauce is best made with fresh tomatoes, but works well with canned plum tomatoes.

INGREDIENTS

Serves 4

60ml/4 tbsp olive oil

1 onion, very finely chopped

1 garlic clove, finely chopped

450g/1lb tomatoes, fresh or canned, chopped with their juice

a few fresh basil leaves or parsley sprigs

salt and ground black pepper

1 Heat the oil in a medium saucepan. Add the onion, and cook over a moderate heat until it is translucent, 5–8 minutes.

2 Stir in the garlic and the tomatoes with their juice (add 45ml/3 tbsp of water if you are using fresh tomatoes). Season with salt and pepper. Add the herbs. Cook for 20–30 minutes.

3 Pass the sauce through a food mill or purée in a blender or food processor. To serve, reheat gently, correct the seasoning and pour over drained pasta.

Special Tomato Sauce

The tomatoes in this sauce are enhanced by the addition of extra vegetables. It is good served with all types of pasta.

INGREDIENTS

Serves 6

700g/1⅔lb tomatoes, fresh or canned, chopped

1 carrot, chopped

1 celery stick, chopped

1 onion, chopped

1 garlic clove, crushed

75ml/5 tbsp olive oil

a few fresh basil leaves or small pinch dried oregano

salt and ground black pepper

1 Place all the ingredients in a medium heavy saucepan, and simmer for 30 minutes.

2 Purée the sauce in a blender or food processor; alternatively press through a sieve.

3 Return the sauce to the pan, correct the seasoning, and bring to a simmer. Cook for about 15 minutes, then pour over drained cooked pasta.

COOK'S TIP

This sauce may be spooned into freezer bags and frozen until required. Allow to thaw at room temperature before reheating.

Spaghetti with Olives and Capers

This spicy sauce originated in the Naples area. It can be quickly assembled using a few store-cupboard ingredients.

Serves 4

60ml/4 tbsp olive oil

2 garlic cloves, finely chopped

small piece of dried red chilli, crumbled

50g/2oz can anchovy fillets, chopped

350g/12oz tomatoes, fresh or
   canned, chopped

115g/4oz/1 cup stoned black olives

30ml/2 tbsp capers, rinsed

15ml/1 tbsp tomato purée

400g/14oz spaghetti

30ml/2 tbsp chopped fresh parsley

1 Heat the oil in a large frying pan. Add the garlic and the dried red chilli, and cook for 2–3 minutes until the garlic is just golden.

2 Add the chopped anchovies, and mash them into the garlic with a fork.

3 Add the fresh or canned tomatoes, olives, capers and tomato purée. Stir well and cook over a moderate heat.

4 Cook the spaghetti in plenty of boiling salted water until *al dente*. Drain well.

5 Turn the spaghetti into the sauce. Increase the heat and cook for 3–4 minutes, turning the pasta constantly. Sprinkle with parsley and serve at once.

Pasta Spirals with Lentils and Cheese

This surprising combination works extremely well.

INGREDIENTS

Serves 4

15ml/1 tbsp olive oil

1 onion, chopped

1 garlic clove, chopped

1 carrot, cut into matchsticks

350g/12oz pasta spirals, such as fusilli

65g/2½oz/½ cup green lentils, boiled for 25 minutes

15ml/1 tbsp tomato purée

15ml/1 tbsp chopped fresh oregano

150ml/¼ pint/⅔ cup vegetable stock

225g/8oz/2 cups grated Cheddar cheese

salt and ground black pepper

freshly grated cheese, to serve

1 Heat the oil in a large frying pan and fry the onion and garlic for 3 minutes. Add the carrot and cook for a further 5 minutes.

COOK'S TIP

Tomato purée is sold in small cans and tubes. If you use a can for this small amount, you can keep the remainder fresh by transferring it to a bowl, covering it with a thin layer of olive oil and putting it in the fridge until needed.

2 Cook the pasta in plenty of boiling salted water according to the instructions on the packet.

3 Add the lentils, tomato purée and oregano to the frying pan, stir, cover and cook for 3 minutes.

4 Add the stock and salt and pepper to the pan. Cover and simmer for 10 minutes. Add the grated Cheddar cheese.

5 Drain the pasta thoroughly and stir into the sauce to coat. Serve with plenty of extra grated cheese.

Greek Pasta with Avocado Sauce

This is an unusual sauce with a pale green colour, studded with red tomato. It has a luxurious, velvety texture. The sauce is rather rich, so you don't need too much of it.

INGREDIENTS

Serves 6

3 ripe tomatoes

2 large ripe avocados

25g/1oz/2 tbsp butter, plus extra for
    tossing the pasta

1 garlic clove, crushed

350ml/12fl oz/1½ cups double cream

dash of Tabasco sauce

450g/1lb green tagliatelle

salt and ground black pepper

freshly grated Parmesan cheese, to garnish

60ml/4 tbsp soured cream, to garnish

1 Halve the tomatoes and remove the cores. Squeeze out the seeds and dice the flesh. Set aside until required.

2 Halve the avocados, remove the stones and peel. Roughly chop the flesh. If hard-skinned, scoop out the flesh with a spoon.

3 Melt the butter in a saucepan and add the garlic. Cook for 1 minute, then add the cream and chopped avocados. Increase the heat, stirring constantly to break up the avocados.

4 Add the diced tomatoes and season to taste with salt, pepper and a little Tabasco sauce. Keep the mixture warm.

5 Cook the pasta in plenty of boiling salted water according to the instructions on the packet. Drain well through a colander and toss with a knob of butter.

6 Divide the pasta among four warmed bowls and spoon over the sauce. Sprinkle with grated Parmesan cheese and top with a spoonful of soured cream.

Tagliatelle with Peas, Asparagus and Beans

A creamy pea sauce makes a wonderful combination with crunchy young vegetables.

INGREDIENTS

Serves 4

15ml/1 tbsp olive oil

1 garlic clove, crushed

6 spring onions, sliced

225g/8oz/2 cups frozen peas, thawed

350g/12oz fresh young asparagus

30ml/2 tbsp chopped fresh sage, plus extra leaves to garnish

finely grated rind of 2 lemons

450ml/¾ pint/1¾ cups vegetable stock or water

225g/8oz/2 cups frozen broad beans, thawed

450g/1lb tagliatelle

60ml/4 tbsp low-fat natural yogurt

1 Heat the oil in a pan. Add the garlic and spring onions and cook gently for 2–3 minutes.

2 Add the peas and 115g/4oz of the asparagus, together with the sage, lemon rind and stock or water. Bring to the boil, reduce the heat and simmer for 10 minutes until tender. Purée in a blender or food processor until smooth.

3 Meanwhile remove the outer skins from the thawed broad beans and discard.

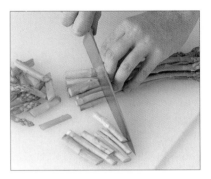

4 Cut the remaining asparagus into 5cm/2in lengths, trimming off any fibrous stems, and blanch in boiling water for 2 minutes.

5 Cook the tagliatelle in plenty of boiling salted water according to the instructions on the packet until *al dente*. Drain well.

6 Add the cooked asparagus and shelled beans to the sauce and reheat. Stir in the yogurt and toss into the tagliatelle. Garnish with sage leaves and serve at once.

Linguine with Sweet Pepper and Cream

*The sweetness of red onion comple-
ments the peppers in this dish.*

INGREDIENTS

Serves 4

1 orange pepper, cored, seeded and cubed

1 yellow pepper, cored, seeded and cubed

1 red pepper, cored, seeded and cubed

350g/12oz linguine

30ml/2 tbsp olive oil

1 red onion, sliced

1 garlic clove, chopped

30ml/2 tbsp chopped fresh rosemary

150ml/¼ pint/⅔ cup double cream

salt and ground black pepper

fresh rosemary sprigs, to garnish

5 Heat the oil in a frying pan and fry the onion and garlic for about 5 minutes until softened.

6 Stir in the sliced peppers and chopped rosemary and fry gently for about 5 minutes until heated through.

7 Stir in the cream and heat through gently. Season to taste with salt and pepper.

8 Drain the pasta thoroughly and toss in the sauce. Serve immediately, garnished with sprigs of fresh rosemary.

1 Preheat the grill to hot. Place the peppers, skin-side up, on a grill rack. Grill for 5–10 minutes until the skins begin to blister and char, turning occasionally.

2 Remove the peppers from the heat, cover with a clean dish towel and leave to stand for about 5 minutes.

3 Carefully peel away the skins from the peppers and discard. Slice the peppers into thin strips.

4 Cook the pasta in plenty of boiling salted water according to the instructions on the packet.

Fusilli with Mascarpone and Spinach

This creamy, green sauce tossed in lightly cooked pasta is best served with plenty of sun-dried tomato ciabatta bread.

INGREDIENTS

Serves 4

350g/12oz pasta spirals, such as fusilli

50g/2oz/¼ cup butter

1 onion, chopped

1 garlic clove, chopped

30ml/2 tbsp fresh thyme leaves

225g/8oz frozen spinach leaves, thawed

225g/8oz/1 cup mascarpone cheese

salt and ground black pepper

fresh thyme sprigs, to garnish

1 Cook the pasta in plenty of boiling salted water according to the instructions on the packet.

2 Melt the butter in a large saucepan and fry the onion for 10 minutes until softened.

3 Stir in the garlic, fresh thyme, spinach and seasoning and heat gently for about 5 minutes, stirring occasionally, until heated through.

4 Stir in the mascarpone cheese and cook gently until heated through. Do not boil.

5 Drain the pasta thoroughly and stir into the sauce. Toss until well coated. Serve immediately, garnished with fresh thyme.

> ### COOK'S TIP
> ❧
> Mascarpone is a rich Italian cream cheese. If you cannot find any, use ordinary full-fat cream cheese instead.

Curly Lasagne with Classic Tomato Sauce

A classic sauce that is simply delicious with any pasta.

INGREDIENTS

Serves 4

30ml/2 tbsp olive oil

1 onion, chopped

30ml/2 tbsp tomato purée

5ml/1 tsp paprika

2 × 400g/14oz cans chopped
 tomatoes, drained

pinch of dried oregano

300ml/½ pint/1¼ cups dry red wine

large pinch of caster sugar

350g/12oz curly lasagne

salt and ground black pepper

Parmesan cheese shavings, to serve

chopped fresh flat leaf parsley, to garnish

1 Heat the oil in a large frying pan and fry the onion for 10 minutes, stirring occasionally, until softened. Add the tomato purée and paprika and cook for a further 3 minutes.

2 Add the tomatoes, oregano, wine and sugar and season to taste, then bring to the boil.

3 Simmer for 20 minutes until the sauce has reduced and thickened, stirring occasionally.

4 Meanwhile, cook the pasta in plenty of boiling salted water according to the instructions on the packet. Drain thoroughly and turn into a large serving dish. Pour over the sauce and toss to coat. Serve sprinkled with Parmesan cheese shavings and the chopped fresh flat leaf parsley.

COOK'S TIP

If you cannot find curly lasasgne use plain lasagne snipped in half lengthways.

Pasta with Roasted Pepper and Tomato

Add other vegetables such as French beans or courgettes or even chick-peas to make this sauce more substantial, if you like.

INGREDIENTS

Serves 4

2 red peppers

2 yellow peppers

45ml/3 tbsp olive oil

1 onion, sliced

2 garlic cloves, crushed

2.5ml/½ tsp mild chilli powder

400g/14oz can chopped tomatoes

450g/1lb dried pasta shells or spirals

salt and ground black pepper

freshly grated Parmesan cheese, to serve

1 Preheat the oven to 200°C/ 400°/Gas 6. Place the peppers on a baking sheet or in a roasting tin and bake for about 20 minutes or until they are beginning to char. Alternatively you could grill the peppers, turning frequently until evenly blistered.

2 Rub the skins off the peppers under cold water. Halve, seed and roughly chop the flesh.

3 Heat the oil in a medium saucepan and add the onion and garlic. Cook gently for 5 minutes until soft and golden.

4 Stir in the chilli powder, cook for 2 minutes, then add the tomatoes and peppers. Bring to the boil and simmer for 10–15 minutes until the sauce is slightly thickened and reduced. Season.

5 Cook the pasta in plenty of boiling salted water according to the instructions on the packet. Drain well and toss with the sauce. Serve piping hot with plenty of grated Parmesan cheese.

Index

Cùil Lodair   Culloden

Contents

Introduction: *debunking the myths of Culloden*

The windy upland plain of Drummossie Moor lies five miles to the east of Inverness. It was here on 16 April 1746 that the battle of Culloden was fought. On one side was the Jacobite army, determined to reclaim the thrones of Britain and Ireland for its Stuart king, and on the other was the army of the British government, equally determined to quash its opponents.

Surviving accounts of Culloden present many different views of what happened at the battle and of its consequences, as propaganda merges with history and fact with fiction. Many believe that Culloden was a war between Scotland's Highlanders and Lowlanders; others hold that it was a battle between the Scots and the English. Some believe that the Jacobite army was little more than an unruly rabble, while others consider that Culloden was the direct cause of the Highland Clearances. Yet none of these is true.

For the last two centuries Culloden's key protagonist, Charles Edward Stuart, has been romanticised and fictionalised as 'Bonnie Prince Charlie', the undisputed hero who appeared in Scotland to lead the brave Highlanders against their Hanoverian government oppressor. His opponent in battle, the Duke of Cumberland, was labelled 'the butcher' for his treatment of the Jacobites at and after the battle of Culloden. These two figures, pitted against each other, have become in some accounts little more than caricatures. The truth is more complex – but no less dramatic and shocking.

Culloden was the last full-scale battle to be fought on British soil and the culmination of the last Jacobite Rising. Its result was not a foregone conclusion: until Culloden the Jacobites had fought this particular campaign undefeated and their army, like the British army, was composed of both professional and non-professional soldiers. While perhaps two-thirds of the Jacobite army at Culloden were Highland Gaels, the rest came from the Scottish Lowlands, France, Ireland and England. Likewise within the Highlands, many major clans supported the British government. The impact of Culloden was all the more devastating as it not only set clan against clan, but divided families, pitting father against son, husband against wife and brother against brother.

Culloden is a battle traditionally associated exclusively with the Highlands – yet its origins lie in Continental Europe.

It was part of a much larger global war. The battle itself was over within one hour, but its repercussions, particularly on the Gaelic culture of the Highlands, were felt for many generations. Yet Highland life had already begun to change. Culloden's aftermath accelerated the dismantling of the clan system and gave a foretaste of what was to come with the Highland Clearances, when many Gaels were forced from their land.

Setting the Scene

'Mourn, hapless Caledonia, mourn
Thy banish'd peace, thy laurels torn!
Thy sons, for valour long renown'd,
Lie slaughter'd on their native ground.'

Tobias Smollett, *The Tears of Scotland*, 1746

'... a young man, not generally esteemed of
considerable character or parts, should land
in a corner of the Island,... and in six
months time,... have seized on the capital
city of Scotland,... it is... dreadful and
amazing... that the work of so many wise
and honest men,... should be in danger
of being overwhelmed by the bursting of
a cloud, which seemed at first gathering,
no bigger than a man's hand.'

P C Yorke, *The Life and Correspondence of Philip Yorke,
Earl of Hardwicke, Lord High Chancellor of Great Britain*

A century of conflict

The seeds of the conflict that culminated at Culloden had been sown during the previous 100 years: a time of religious and political upheaval. When the Stuart King James VI died in 1625, having united the crowns of Scotland and England in 1603, his son Charles I inherited the throne and with it an English Parliament in deep disagreement over foreign policy. His marriage to the Roman Catholic French princess Henrietta Maria and his preference for the formal rituals of the Church of England were unpopular, particularly with the Scots. In 1637 his ill-advised attempt to impose the Book of Common Prayer in Scotland provoked uproar: many Scots saw it as a threat to the freedom of their Church and to their Presbyterian principles. The National Covenant, drawn up in 1638 and circulated throughout the country, was enthusiastically signed by those opposing the king's ecclesiastical policies.

In January 1649 King Charles was tried for treason, found guilty and condemned to be put to death *'by the severing of his head from his body'*. England was declared a republic, but the Scots accepted Charles I's son as king of both Scotland and England, and crowned him Charles II at Scone in 1651. Oliver Cromwell responded by advancing into Scotland, defeating the royalist troops at Dunbar. Then he pursued them into England, crushing them decisively at Worcester in September 1651. Charles was forced into exile on the Continent.

Almost a decade later, England restored its monarchy, but Charles II's reign was soon marked by intense religious division, as he attempted to introduce toleration of Roman Catholics and Protestant Dissenters. Anti-Catholicism was widespread and the 1673 Test Act went so far as to exclude Roman Catholics from both

From top of page:

Contemporary engraving of Scottish worshippers protesting at the form of church service imposed by Charles I; portrait of Charles II by an unknown artist; James VII of Scotland and II of England by an unknown artist, c1690

Houses of Parliament. In 1677, partly in an effort to re-establish his own Protestant credentials, Charles II arranged the marriage of his niece, Mary, to the Protestant prince William of Orange.

When Charles died in 1685, his younger brother James, aged fifty-one and a convert to Catholicism, succeeded to the throne peacefully to become James VII of Scotland and II of England & Ireland. Three years later his Catholic wife, Mary of Modena, gave birth to a son, James Francis Edward Stuart, and it seemed that a Roman Catholic dynasty could soon be a reality. But before the baby was five months old, the king's nephew, William of Orange, landed a large army in England to popular support. As the king's own disaffected army and navy gradually deserted to join forces with William, James fled to France.

Mary and William ascended the throne in 1689 as joint monarchs and defenders of Protestantism. In Scotland, however, where Stuart monarchs had ruled for over 300 years, loyalty to the deposed James remained strong. A Convention in Edinburgh decided that the Scottish government should back William of Orange. But many Scots – including more Protestants than Catholics – continued to support the exiled James, believing him to be the legally constituted king.

Left to right:
John Graham of Claverhouse, 1st Viscount of Dundee, by an unknown artist; William of Orange and his wife Mary by Sir Peter Lely, 1677

The date 16 April 1689 marked the start of the first Jacobite Rising, when John Graham of Claverhouse, 1st Viscount of Dundee, raised the exiled King James's Standard on the hilltop of Dundee Law. Two hundred Irish troops landed at Kintyre to join him and gradually he gained support from those Highland clans who were Catholic or Episcopalian (favouring a system of church government by bishops). On 27 July 1689 Dundee's army of 2,500 men met the 4,000-strong government troops led by General Hugh Mackay at the Pass of Killiecrankie. The Jacobites emerged victorious but about one-third of the Highland force was killed and Dundee himself was fatally wounded. A series of government expeditions to subdue the Highlands followed. Two years later the Jacobites were forced to agree to a truce and in January 1692 they formally surrendered to the government. However, the state-sanctioned massacre of members of the MacDonald clan in Glencoe in February 1692 soured attitudes among many Highlanders towards the new regime.

When William of Orange died in 1702, the throne passed to Anne, James VII's daughter, a Protestant. Her reign was dominated by war in Europe and, in its early years, by conflict between the English and Scottish parliaments. Scotland's

Right:

The Battle of Glenshiel, a contemporary painting by Peter Tillemans. The government's defeat of Jacobite and Spanish troops here on 10 June ended the 1719 Jacobite Rising

Below:

George I by Sir Godfrey Kneller, 1714 and (bottom) George II by Thomas Hudson, 1744

economy was faltering and widespread discontent gave the Jacobites hope that James Stuart would gain power when Queen Anne died with no immediate successor. But the English Act of Settlement of 1701 required the monarch to be Protestant and so the crown passed to Anne's second cousin, the Elector of Hanover: King George I. However, the Stuart claim to the Crown would linger on for another century.

As the nearest Protestant heir according to the Act of Settlement, George I became the first of the Hanoverian kings. He aligned himself with the Whigs, a loose political party who had previously opposed the succession of the Catholic King James VII and II, and who now formed the government.

George I had reigned for less than a year when he was faced in 1715 with a Jacobite rebellion. The Jacobites sought to put James Francis Edward Stuart, known to his opponents as 'the Pretender', on the throne. But the rebellion lacked strategic initiative and was checked by government troops. Faced with defeat, James was forced back to France, never to return to Scotland.

In 1719 the Jacobites mounted a second rebellion. This time, they secured the support of Spain, but storms at sea prevented all but 300 Spanish troops arriving in Scotland. Attempts to recruit Scottish soldiers raised an army of around 1,000 men but they were too poorly equipped to defeat government troops.

On George I's death in 1727, his son was crowned King George II and, like his father, he too faced a Jacobite threat. This time, however, the Rising of 1745 ('The Forty-Five'), under the leadership of Charles Edward Stuart, would give the government rather more cause for concern. By 1745, political infighting, charges of corruption at home and military setbacks abroad were beginning to undermine the authority of the Whig government. The Jacobite Rising of 1745 took the government by surprise.

Life in Scotland:
the background to the Forty-Five

The rise of the House of Hanover had not achieved peace and prosperity. In Europe, there continued to be political unrest over religion, succession, influence and empires, and the British army was involved in a round of wars on the Continent against the major powers of Europe. In Scotland there was economic hardship for many, exacerbated by poor harvests in the 1690s and by trade competition from England. The attempt to set up a Scottish trading colony in the New World, known as the Darien Venture, proved disastrous. It floundered largely because the English colonial governors in North America and the West Indies refused to sell supplies to the second expedition to Darien in 1700. Scotland was already reliant on an economic relationship with England: in 1700 half of Scotland's exports went to England, although this figure began to decline in the early years of the eighteenth century.

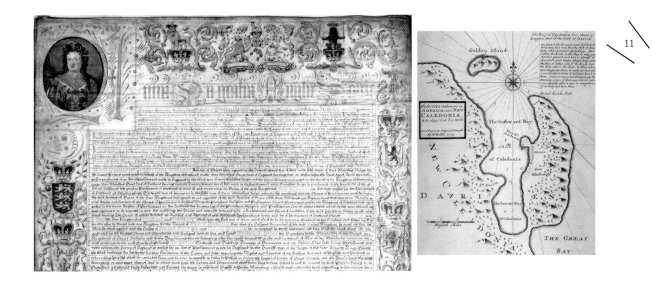

Above left:

Act of Parliament ratifying the Treaty of Union between the Scottish and English parliaments in 1707

Above right:

A map of 1699 by Herman Moll, showing the site of the Scottish trading colony in Darien, Panama

The Act of Union in 1707 saw the two kingdoms accept one parliament, one sovereign, one coinage, one system of taxation and one trading regime, although the Scottish legal system and the Scottish Church remained separate. But for some the Union failed to deliver the economic prosperity it had promised. Lowland cities in Scotland, such as Edinburgh and Glasgow, were prospering, but much of the Highlands was not, increasingly subjected to ever greater economic and social pressures. Economic changes, frequently led by clan chiefs, resulted in the break-up of systems of tenure and methods of landholding. Land rents were increased, hitting the Highlanders hard: for some the only way out was to emigrate overseas.

Resentment against the government was also fuelled by the oppressive system of military roads, bridges and forts, built to keep the Highlanders in check. Some leading Scots turned to the Stuarts again because they thought the British state had failed to share the profits from its empire. But for the resurgent Jacobites to succeed, support from Europe was vital. The Scottish Jacobites could count on their 'auld alliance' with France, built on centuries of joint interests in controlling England's expansion plans. In 1744 Anglo-French rivalry finally erupted into war, and factions in the French government were keen to exploit Jacobite plotting: a co-ordinated rising and invasion would surely deliver the enemy a knockout blow.

The Jacobites had proved willing to fight for their cause in the Risings of 1715 and 1719 in support of James VII's son, James Francis Edward Stuart. These had been unsuccessful, but now fresh hope came in the shape of James Stuart's son and heir, the 20-year old Charles Edward Stuart.

A map of the central Highlands of Scotland, published in 1746, showing the network of military roads constructed by General Wade between 1725 and 1736

Who were the Jacobites?

Jacobitism was the political movement dedicated to restoring the Stuart kings to the thrones of Scotland and England. The Jacobites took their name from the Latin form of James, *Jacobus*, after their deposed king James VII.

People became Jacobites for all sorts of reasons. Many embraced Jacobitism because they believed the Stuarts to be the lawful kings; for others it was a principled refusal to accept Parliament's right to decide British royal succession. Many Catholics hoped the Stuarts would end discriminatory laws, while others resented what they saw as English domination. Many were Scottish patriots who opposed the 1707 Act of Union. Some were motivated by intense family loyalties, while others were simply swept up in the adventure. Whilst the majority of Jacobite support came from Highland and Lowland Scotland, there were also English, Irish and French Jacobites.

The Baptism of Prince Charles Edward Stuart at the Muti Palace, Rome, by Antonio David, 1725. Charles was to rejuvenate the Jacobite cause

Local battle and global war:
Culloden and the international balance of power

The Battle of Fontenoy, 11 May 1745, by Pierre Lenfant (1704–87). Louis XV is shown indicating the victorious commander, the Marshal de Saxe

The battle of Culloden has always been understood as a very Highland event. The exact figures will never be known for certain, but approximately 67 per cent of Jacobites at Culloden were Highland Gaels – and militias from Argyll fought on the government side, a fact that is too often forgotten. Though it was the last pitched battle fought on British soil, and thus of tremendous national significance, its aftermath is usually linked to the troubled history of the Highlands, and to the intensification of economic and social processes that eventually resulted in the Highland Clearances. Viewing Culloden in terms of Highland history is only right and proper: but it is not the only way of understanding its causes and consequences. The battle was also an important part of a sequence of imperial conflicts that spanned the globe during the mid-eighteenth century.

The immediate origins of the 1745 Rising can be found not in the Highlands but in a British military defeat in what is now Belgium. On 11 May 1745 an allied army comprising British, Dutch, Hanoverian and Austrian regiments was beaten decisively by the French at Fontenoy. It is one of the ironies of history that the defeated army's commander was none other than William, Duke of Cumberland. It is perhaps pushing the point too far to argue that Cumberland was thus partly responsible for the outbreak of the Forty-Five. But it could legitimately be held that Cumberland's burning desire to crush the Jacobites stemmed, at least in part, from a realisation that his military failure had contributed to Charles Edward Stuart's expedition to Scotland. The Duke's draconian policies after Culloden were certainly shaped by his wish to return to Flanders and reverse the French onslaught against the Austrian Netherlands and Dutch Republic, which his own defeat at Fontenoy had enabled.

Placing Culloden in its wider European context casts some of the battle's most famous figures in a radically different light. Cumberland, viewed in this way, emerges not as the military hero who made the government's victory inevitable, but as a fallible commander who invariably struggled against armies of equal size, equipment and training.

That the Rising was an integral part of the larger war in Europe is clear from the cosmopolitan nature of those involved – French, Irish, Hanoverians, Hessians and Dutch all played a greater or lesser part in the campaign. This international profile shows how Highland clanship could still make an impact on the European stage, even though, as France and Hanover indirectly fought out their foreign policy objectives in the region, the effect was far from positive. The political and mental horizons of the Highlands were in no way parochial or insular, and the region was, and strived to remain, engaged with the main military, political and religious issues of the time.

But it is not just events on the European continent that should inform our understanding of the 1745 Rising, its bloody conclusion and its consequences. Culloden was part of a global war fought in countries and on oceans far removed from the Highlands of Scotland.

Across the Atlantic in June 1745, only weeks before Charles Edward Stuart arrived in Scotland, Royal Navy warships, together with New England militia units, took the great French fortress of Louisbourg which protected the Gulf of St Lawrence. The French understood the importance of the defeat only too well. Faced with depleting their army in the Low Countries in order either to retake Louisbourg or support the Jacobites, the French initially marshalled an invasion force to support the Stuart army in England. However, the Jacobite retreat from Derby ensured that French priorities switched quickly to the recovery of territory in North America. By the spring of 1746, 11,000 French troops were already being sent across the Atlantic, denying any hope of substantial reinforcements to the Jacobites just when they needed them most. There were many turning points in the Forty-Five: the failure to secure Scotland after Prestonpans, the Derby Council, and the decision to stand and fight at Culloden. Yet indirectly the Rising was also shaped by events in North America as France struggled to hold her empire together – just as Britain was later to do.

Soon after the French lost their key base in Louisbourg, Britain suffered a similar blow

– but on the other side of the world. In September 1746, only five months after Culloden, the French took Madras, the English East India Company's main base in southern India. In the peace of 1748 between Britain and France, Louisbourg and Madras were exchanged, thus preserving the status

quo ante. But the balance of power had changed, and Culloden was the cause of that change. With the liquidation of Jacobitism as a military force, France could never again sponsor domestic insurrection within Britain in an effort to tie down British military and naval strength at home.

Culloden changed imperial power relations in one other hugely important respect. With the final pacification of the Highlands, the region's manpower could be redeployed for empire-building purposes. Highland regiments were not only used in the Seven Years War (French-Indian War) and the American Revolutionary conflict, but – within fourteen months of Culloden – as imperial cannon fodder. In 1747 the British War Office authorised the recruitment of 600 Scots for service in India. The officers were informed that the men *'be composed of Rebels and they* [The War Office] *declared they will accept of any man fit for service without enquiring into his former life'.*

Above:

The Capture of Louisbourg, 28 June 1745, by Peter Monamy (1681-1749)

14

The intention, of course, was to dispose of former rebels in ways that benefited the national interest. But in defeat many Jacobite families showed a degree of political astuteness and tenacity which had been spectacularly lacking during the Forty-Five itself. In 1756 Simon Fraser of Lovat, the son of the executed Lord Lovat, raised a Highland regiment that served with distinction in Canada. In that unit were many ex-Jacobite kindreds beginning the long, hard process of re-ingratiating themselves with the British state.

If the process of fighting for forgiveness began with the Seven Years War, it reached its zenith during Britain's long and bitter conflict against her American colonists between 1775 and 1783. Simon Fraser of Lovat once again raised a regiment, as did representatives of the Macphersons of Cluny and Mackenzies of Cromartie. Again, the ironies of history are obvious. Like the 1745 Rising, the American War of Independence had many of the characteristics of a civil war. Once again, too, many Jacobites found themselves on the losing side, backing Britain's vain attempt to hold her North American empire.

Final defeat for the British came at Yorktown in Virginia in October 1781. But this was not without its benefits for ex-Jacobite families and thousands of ordinary Gaels, whose loyalty and effort was recognised by the British state. The erstwhile chiefs had their ancestral estates returned to them in 1784, while Highland soldiers gained land and security in Nova Scotia and Canada. Britain's loss in America served, therefore, to wipe away the sins of the past. Viewed from an international perspective, Culloden is framed by two catastrophic British defeats 36 years apart and far removed from the bleak moors outside Inverness. But if Fontenoy marked the road to Culloden, Yorktown brought redemption.

Andrew Mackillop

James Francis Edward Stuart

Known as:	The Old Pretender, James VIII and III
Born:	10 June 1688, St James's Palace, London
Died:	1 January 1766, Rome
Buried:	St Peter's Basilica, the Vatican, Rome
Father:	James VII
Mother:	Mary of Modena
Married:	3 September 1719 to Maria Clementina Sobieski, daughter of the Polish king, John III Sobieski
Children:	Charles Edward Stuart and Henry Benedict Stuart
Image:	Portrait of Prince James Francis Edward Stuart by an unknown artist

Charles Edward Stuart

Known as:	Bonnie Prince Charlie, The Young Pretender
Born:	31 December 1720, Rome
Died:	31 January 1788, Rome
Buried:	First in the Cathedral of Frascati, where his brother was a bishop. On his brother's death, Charles's remains were moved to the crypt of St Peter's Basilica, the Vatican, Rome
Father:	James Francis Edward Stuart
Mother:	Maria Clementina Sobieski
Married:	28 March 1772 to Princess Louise of Stolberg-Gedern
Children:	Charlotte, Duchess of Albany, born 1753 to his mistress Clementina Walkinshaw
Image:	Portrait of Prince Charles Edward Stuart in 1729 by Antonio David

The Government versus the Jacobite Cause

'I am come home Sir.'

Prince Charles's retort to Alexander Macdonald of Boisdale,
who told him to go home after Charles had landed in Eriskay, 1745.

'Certainly France sees we have drained our country of troops to reinforce the army in Flanders and knows no more effectual way to make us recall 'em than by playing the Pretender upon us.'

Joseph Yorke, Lieutenant-Colonel of the government's 1st Regiment of Foot, fighting in Flanders, on hearing of the Prince's arrival in Scotland.

The Prince's decision

Top of page:

Prince Charles Edward Stuart, painted by Domenico Duprà on the eve of his departure from France in 1745

18

The timing of the Jacobite Rising was determined to a large extent by international affairs. By 1744, after a long period of friendly co-existence, Britain's relations with France had deteriorated to the point of open war. King Louis XV of France planned a large-scale invasion of southern England early in 1744. This was to be a surprise attack with Charles Edward Stuart as its political figurehead.

As rumours of the French invasion reached them, the British government imposed a crackdown on Jacobite suspects in England. British regiments were withdrawn from Flanders, ready to respond to any attack by the French. But the weather, again, was against the invaders: in late February a fierce storm scattered the French fleet, sinking one ship and putting a further five out of action. The French government called off the project and gradually withdrew support from Charles. With the immediate threat over, the British government turned its attention to other matters.

The following year, on 11 May 1745, the French inflicted the first of a series of defeats on the British army in Flanders at the battle of Fontenoy, where they defeated the British forces led by the Duke of Cumberland, King George II's son. During the battle, Irish Jacobite troops fought with the French while Highlanders of the Black Watch regiment served with the Duke on the side of Britain. George II spent the summer in Hanover, an ill-advised absence that fuelled the increasing discontent with his regime at home. The military focus on the Continent left Britain exposed and Charles saw his chance. By raising enough support for the Jacobite cause, he hoped to persuade the French to reactivate their plans for an invasion of England. He knew that this was probably his only chance.

O hì-rì-rì, tha e tighinn,
O hì-rì-rì, 'n Rìgh tha uainn,
Gheibheamaid ar n-airm 's ar n-èideadh,
'S breacan an fhèilidh an cuaich.

O hì-rì-rì, he is coming,
O hì-rì-rì, our exiled King,
Let us take our arms and clothing,
And the flowing tartan plaid.

The Prince sets sail

Òran don Phrionnsa,
Alasdair mac Mhaighstir
Alasdair; *A Song to
the Prince,* Alexander
MacDonald.

After the ill-fated initiative of 1744 Prince Charles continued to badger French ministers for commitment to another invasion. But this was not forthcoming. So in secret, and without the knowledge or support of his father, the Prince developed a plan to assemble an armed expedition in spring 1745. Charles knew it was impossible to land in England without an army, so he decided to sail for Scotland where he had been told numerous supporters would welcome him. Funded by Jacobite benefactors, he fitted out a small frigate, the *Du Teillay*, and a larger man-of-war, the *Elisabeth*, under the pretence that this was a normal privateering cruise. Before he departed Charles wrote to Louis XV:

'*Having tried in vain by every means to meet Your Majesty in the hope of getting, out of your generosity, the help I need to enable me to play a role worthy of my birth, I have resolved to make myself known by my deeds and on my own to undertake a project which would be certain to succeed with a moderate amount of help.*'

Such help would be crucial if the Rising was to be a success, for France was one of only a handful of western European powers with the military and naval muscle capable of forcing the restoration of the Stuart monarchs.

Left to right:
Action at Sea, 9 July 1745,
by Harold Wylie; Prince
Charles Edward taking
leave of Antoine Walsh
at Loch nan Uamh, by an
unknown artist, *c*1745.
The Prince is giving Walsh
letters for his father, James

In 1744 a small number of Scottish Highland clan chieftains had promised that they would rise if Prince Charles arrived with as few as 3,000 French troops. Charles had raised far fewer men: nevertheless his ships, loaded with weapons, supplies and money, set sail for Scotland on 5 July 1745. But only five days after leaving France they were attacked by a Royal Navy warship, HMS *Lion*. Both the *Lion* and the Jacobites' *Elisabeth* were badly damaged and had to limp back to their home ports. Remaining undetected aboard the *Du Teillay*, Charles pressed on. And on 23 July 1745 he landed with a handful of supporters and seven close companions on the island of Eriskay in the Outer Hebrides.

'Long live King James VIII and Charles Prince of Wales; prosperity to Scotland and no Union!'

The shout that went up from clansmen at Glenfinnan after the assembly of the clans, the proclamation of King James and the reading of the commission to Charles as Prince Regent.

Raising the Standard

20

Convinced that the British were longing for him to liberate them from Hanoverian oppression, the Prince was astonished when first one clan chief and then another told him to go home. Determined not to retreat, he sailed to the mainland, arriving on 25 July. Prince Charles may have had few weapons and fewer troops, but what he did have was charisma, charm and persistence, all vital qualities in winning over the hesitant clan chiefs. Charles was also liberal with the truth, saying that the French king had agreed to send substantial aid and that English Jacobites had pledged to rise for him. Neither of these promises was true.

The clan chiefs were uneasy about the lack of French assistance, without which, many believed, the Rising was doomed to fail. Times had moved on, too: in the past the Highlands' geographical and cultural remoteness coupled with political and economic isolation had made many clan chiefs active Jacobites with the power to summon up large numbers of fighting men. But now the political climate had changed and fewer Highland chiefs were willing to risk everything to change their king. Charles attempted to appeal to their sense of honour and duty to his cause. To the initially sceptical and highly influential Donald Cameron of Lochiel he guaranteed a French pension worth the same as his Highland estate, or a commission in the French army of equal value. When Lochiel promised his support other chiefs began to come in too. Some were drawn to the political promises the Prince made, including abolishing the Union and proclaiming religious freedom. On 19 August 1745, before about 1,200 men, Charles raised his father's Standard at Glenfinnan. The Rising had begun.

Above:

Portrait of Donald Cameron of Lochiel by Sir George Chalmers (c1720-91). Cameron wrote of Prince Charles's arrival in Scotland: 'whoever advised him to undertake itt … has a great deal to answer for'

Top of page:

The monument at Glenfinnan commemorating the site where Charles Edward raised his father's Standard

The Jacobite threat

The Prince's appearance in an area of the Highlands remote from the seat of government meant that it was over a week before the authorities heard of his arrival. Despite widespread unease among government supporters in the Highlands, there was little sense of urgency. Most of the British army was in Flanders and Germany, leaving an inexperienced army of about 4,000 men in Scotland under the British General, Sir John Cope. The Black Watch regiment, traditionally the government's Highland force, had been moved in 1745 to the south of England to help with defence plans against any possible French invasion.

Despite Prince Charles's military experience being limited, he took on the post of commander-in-chief of the Jacobite army. The man who was to have the most influence within the Jacobite army was Lord George Murray, by 1745 in his early 50s. He had supported the Jacobites in the Risings of 1715 and 1719 and had spent several years in exile on the Continent. But in 1724 he had come back to Britain, and the following year was granted a government pardon. Initially sceptical of Charles's chances, Murray visited Sir John Cope, the commander of government troops, in August 1745, and Cope appointed him Deputy Sheriff of Perthshire. But within a month Lord George, apparently driven by his conscience, had changed his allegiance to join the Jacobite army, where he was made a Lieutenant-General. He was to play a crucial role in creating military discipline and order.

Leading his army north into the Highlands, Cope was met with little support. He lacked proper information about the Prince's army and, believing the Jacobite force to be stronger than it really was, he decided to avoid an engagement at the Pass of Corryairack and marched northwards to Inverness. Ironically, the military roads constructed under General Wade to allow the government forces to patrol the Highlands only served to allow the Jacobites easy passage through the country. And with the road clear, the Jacobites marched south, unopposed.

Above:
Caricature of Prince Charles on a government poster of 1745 offering a £30,000 reward for his capture

Below:
Portrait of Lord George Murray by an unknown artist, c1740

The charismatic Prince:
raising recruits

Following his cool welcome on the island of Eriskay, Charles sailed to Arisaig, on the west coast of Scotland, where an enclave of Catholics would protect him. The Prince expected support from Scottish Roman Catholics for a Catholic dynasty, but their number was very small, and in fact he benefited more from discontented Episcopalians and anti-Unionists.

Detail of portrait of Prince Charles Edward by E Gill, c1746-9

But to many in Scotland, Hanoverian rule was preferable to Stuart kingship. Most Scots were Presbyterian and traditionally hostile to the Stuarts, and Charles failed to win them over: 1745 was not a national rising. Jacobite recruiters sometimes used bribery and threats to fill the ranks. In early September Charlotte Robertson, Lady Lude, entertained Prince Charles at Blair Castle, where she held a ball to drum up support. To those who refused to join him, she threatened to seize and carry off their possessions.

22

The Jacobite army existed for barely nine months, most of which was spent in the field. From the outset, it was decided that the whole army would wear at least one tartan item, underlining the differences between the Jacobites and their opposition. On the principle that *'nothing encouraged men more than seeing their officers dressed like themselves and ready to share their fate'*, Lord George Murray insisted that the Jacobite officers donned tartan too.

Lord George Murray		**Sir John Cope**	
Born:	4 October 1694, Huntingtower, near Perth	*Born:*	1690
Died:	11 October 1760, Medemblik, Holland	*Died:*	28 July 1760, London
Occupation:	Jacobite General	*Occupation:*	British General
Father:	John Murray, 1st Duke of Atholl, chief of Clan Murray	*Father:*	Lieutenant-Colonel Henry Cope
Mother:	Catherine, daughter of the 3rd Duke of Hamilton	*Mother:*	Dorothy Waller
Married:	1728 to Amelia, daughter and heiress of James Murray of Strowan and Glencarse	*Married:*	1712 Jane Duncombe; second marriage 1736 to Elizabeth Waple
Children:	Three sons and two daughters	*Children:*	One son, James, by his first wife
Image:	*Lord George Murray,* an ink portrait by Robert Strange	*Image:*	*Sir John Cope,* a sketch of 1751–8 by George Townshend, the only portrait that still exists

Alasdair mac Mhaighstir Alasdair or Alexander MacDonald (1695–1770)

Alexander MacDonald was a Gaelic poet and propagandist. Born near Glenfinnan, he attended Glasgow University and later became a schoolmaster. Shortly before the Jacobite Rising of 1745, he converted to Roman Catholicism. Perhaps in expectation of the Rising, he had already composed a number of Jacobite songs. It is thought that these songs, including *Òran Nuadh* or *A New Song,* were sent to Paris to encourage the Prince before he set sail for Scotland.

When the ship carrying Charles Edward Stuart arrived in Scotland, Alexander MacDonald was among the first to go on board. Dispatched to Ardnamurchan to recruit for the Jacobite cause, he returned with 50 men, and the Prince rewarded him with a commission as Captain in the Clanranald regiment. In August, when the Prince was in Perth, MacDonald was sent to Dundee to raise money in the name of King James. He recalled:

'Being masters of the town we seized 2 vessalls with arms and ammunition, which we sent further up the Tay towards Perth: we likewise took up some Publick money here, … liberated some prisoners and proclaimed the prince regent.'

He was with the Prince on the march south to Edinburgh and fought at the battle of Prestonpans. His account of the aftermath of the battle aimed to dispel the myth of the brutal Highlander:

'I can with the strictest truth and sincerity declare that I often heard our people call out to the soldiers if they wanted quarters, and we the officers exerted our utmost pains to protect the soldiers from their first fury, when either through their stubbornness or want of language they did not cry for quarters, and I observed some of our private men run to P Seton for ale and other liquors to support the wounded.'

Alexander MacDonald went on to fight at Culloden. He survived the battle but his home and possessions were plundered and destroyed and he and his wife and children were forced to keep on the move throughout the Highlands. In later years he published a volume of poems called *The Resurrection of the Ancient Scottish Language.* Containing strong Jacobite sentiments and attacks on the House of Hanover, the poems received equal measures of praise and hostility. He escaped prosecution but unsold copies of the book were seized and publicly burnt by the hangman in Edinburgh. Alexander MacDonald spent the last years of his life on the west coast of Scotland. He died at the age of around 75 and is buried in Arisaig.

Donald Campbell of Airds

Donald Campbell of Airds lived in Appin in the west of Scotland, where he was employed by the Duke of Argyll as his factor. Clan Campbell were traditionally strong government supporters and Donald Campbell of Airds served on the government side. Throughout the campaign he provided important intelligence of Jacobite movements in the west of Scotland. He was one of the first to know about the arrival of the Prince and played a key role in getting the information to Edinburgh, from where it was passed to the government in London. In August 1745, he wrote:

Portrait of Donald Campbell of Airds by an unknown artist

> *'This morning I had an express with very extraordinary news, could it be depended on, viz. that a vessel is landed in Arisaig with between two and three hundred men, and two thousand stand of arms, among whom are the Pretender's eldest son ...'*

By October, the Duke of Argyll had received a royal warrant granting him powers to call out the Argyll militia. Donald Campbell of Airds was commissioned as a Captain of one of the militia companies. The following spring, he was part of an expedition sent to attack the Jacobites just north of Aberdeen. Although the two sides failed to meet, Airds was confident in his men's ability, writing:

> *'It was impossible to show greater keenness and willingness to come up with the enemy, than they did – and I am really persuaded had they opportunity they would fight to a man. This pursuit of the rebels will heighten their spirits, and makes me hope they will do their duty when occasion offers.'*

That occasion occurred two days later, when Argyll's men encountered the Jacobites at Keith in Aberdeenshire. On the evening of 20 March 1746, the Jacobites made a surprise attack on Argyll's men. Airds' militia took refuge in a church. He later recounted:

> *'By this time some four men being killed damped the spirits of those in the church, that they called for quarters [mercy] and were mostly made prisoners ...'*

The so-called 'Skirmish at Keith' badly affected the morale of the militia, but Campbell of Airds went on to command his men at Culloden, which he described as 'A Glorious Day'. After the battle, the Argyll militia were employed in hunting down Jacobites, but Airds was instrumental in ensuring that his men did not participate in the atrocities of the time and he prevented much of the area around Glenfinnan from being destroyed and plundered.

24

'*Follow me gentlemen by the assistance of God I will this day make you a free and happy people.*'

Charles Edward Stuart, before the battle of Prestonpans.

Top of page:
Contemporary cartoon satirising General Cope's flight after his defeat by the Jacobites at Prestonpans on 21 September 1745

Below:
Contemporary etching showing Jacobite troops parading outside the Palace of Holyroodhouse in 1745

Foot of page:
Caricature of Lowland ladies excited at news of the Prince's arrival – one of a series by an unknown member of Sir John Clerk of Penicuik's family. They are now known as 'The Penicuik Sketches'

The Jacobites take Edinburgh

Moving south through Scotland, the Jacobites took Perth on 4 September 1745. But Charles needed money and men. The funds he had arrived with had run out and to keep his army on the road he raised taxes from local citizens in his father's name as the 'rightful king'. With new recruits gathered from Perthshire and elsewhere, the army once more headed south, this time with Edinburgh in its sights. News of the Jacobite army's approach was met with panic in the capital and efforts were made to strengthen the city's defences. But early in the morning of 17 September, when the city gate at the Netherbow Port was opened to let a coach through, the Jacobites rushed the sentries and seized control of the city. The next day the Prince's father was proclaimed King James VIII at the Mercat Cross and a triumphant Charles entered the Palace of Holyroodhouse.

Meanwhile Sir John Cope, heading the government troops, had arrived in Aberdeen, from where he shipped his men and supplies to Dunbar. Arriving on 18 September, Cope found Edinburgh already taken and resolved to fight as soon as possible. The battle that took place at Prestonpans on 21 September was a disaster for Cope and his men, who were skilfully outmanoeuvred by the Jacobites. In less than fifteen minutes the battle was over: hundreds of government soldiers were killed or injured and 1,500 were taken prisoner. To the Jacobites' credit, they observed the rules of war and were merciful towards their wounded and captured opponents.

Following the battle, Prince Charles held court at the Palace of Holyroodhouse for nearly six weeks. During this time he strengthened his army as new recruits arrived from the north, and he set about improving his finances by raising taxes, demanding money from the Royal Bank and selling off goods from the customs houses in Leith. He also wrote to France pleading for a speedy invasion of England. And by the middle of October it looked as if his plea would be answered with the arrival of Alexander du Boyer, unofficial French envoy to the Jacobite court in Scotland, with weapons and money.

To the disappointment of many of his supporters, Charles showed no interest in recalling the old Scottish Parliament. Had he done so, he would have given the rebellion wider political authority. Such an action would also have challenged government claims that a dangerous Stuart dictator was attempting to seize the throne.

The Prince and the Duke:
troops and tactics

'I have the satisfaction to acquaint your Lordship, that His Majesty is taking the necessary measures for having, in a short time, such a number of regular troops in Scotland as may, by the blessing of God, be sufficient to put a speedy end to the present unnatural rebellion.'

The Duke of Newcastle to Lord Milton, the Lord Justice Clerk at Edinburgh, 14 December 1745.

28

A map of 1747 by John Finlayson, entitled *A general map of Great Britain, wherein are delineated the military operations in that island during the years 1745 and 1746 and even the secret Routs of the Pr … after the Battle of Culloden until his Escape to France.* Finlayson served in the Jacobite artillery at Culloden. His reference to Charles as 'Pr …' would mean 'Prince' to a Jacobite reader and 'Pretender' to a government supporter

'The Prince Could not bear to hear any body differ in Sentiment from him, and took a dislike to Every body that did, for he had a Notion of Commanding this army As any General does a body of Mercenaries, and so lett them know only what he pleased, and they obey without inquiring further about the matter.'

Lord Elcho, *A Short Account of the Affairs of Scotland in the Years 1744, 1745, 1746*

The Jacobites set out for England

Whilst at Holyroodhouse Charles formed a Council of War composed of the Jacobite leaders. The Council was to develop a strategy for the Prince's next move, but it was divided. Prince Charles had his eye on England, but the majority of his Council did not share his determination for an invasion.

Some of the leading Jacobites were sceptical about restoring the Stuart king to the throne of England. Their ambitions lay only in Scotland, with the restoration of the Scottish throne, the reinstatement of the Scottish Parliament and the ending of the Union with England. Others who opposed the Prince's plan to invade England argued that the priority should be to secure Scotland first, fearful that otherwise all would be lost. The majority of the Council believed that they had too few men and arms to mount a successful invasion and that, without help from France, embarking on such a course of action would be foolish in the extreme.

Charles, flushed with success, did not wish to hear such arguments. Conscious that they were running out of money and beginning to lose men, the Prince wanted immediate action. He argued forcefully that England was ripe for conquest, that his support in the south was strong and that a French invasion was imminent. Only the last of these assertions contained an element of truth. Whether he was simply misinformed or knowingly dishonest, his determination swayed the Council.

'... *the first great error committed was going to England in the time and manner we did ... To enter into England with betwixt three and four thousand men at a time when they had thirty thousand regular troops and all the militia of England to oppose us and when we had no account of a French landing nor no assurance of being joined by the Country ...*'

Letter from John Roy Stewart to James Edgar, 1747.

The march south

On 3 November, the Jacobite army of around 5,000 to 6,000 men set out for England. The government had used the intervening period to bring back its troops from the Continent and had by now assembled an army under Field-Marshal Wade at Newcastle. Charles wanted to confront them, but on the advice of Lord George Murray they made instead for Carlisle. With the roads clear to the south, the Prince's army made rapid progress: morale in the ranks was high and they were aided by their own fearsome reputation. At Manchester around 250 men formed a regiment, but no other Englishmen joined the Prince. A growing unease among the Jacobite army's commanders was taking hold at the lack of English support. Although curious crowds thronged the streets to see the Prince's army pass, few were willing to join. Charles's promises of an English uprising were sounding hollow.

Lord George Murray and others had argued the folly of leaving Scotland unsecured – and their fears were proved true. As soon as the Jacobites were over the Border, government forces speedily regained control of the central Lowlands, including the city of Edinburgh. At the same time the government raised a militia of 600 men to reinforce Stirling Castle. In the north of Scotland, the government was active too, raising altogether eighteen independent companies from the northern clans loyal to George II. The Jacobites managed to retain control of the north-east of Scotland: the east coast harbours provided excellent opportunities to land men and supplies sent from France. In mid-November, the government anchored its sloop *Hazard* just off Montrose in an attempt to disrupt this supply line. But the Jacobites attacked and the ship's captain was forced to surrender. The Jacobites captured the *Hazard* and renamed it *Le Prince Charles* in honour of their hero.

Above:

Engraving of Stirling Castle from John Slezer's *Theatrum Scotiae*, published in 1693 (detail)

Top of page:

Modern model of the government sloop, the *Hazard*, captured by the Jacobites off Montrose but later recaptured by the Royal Navy

Lady Anne Mackintosh

Born in 1723, Anne Farquharson grew up to be a strong-minded and independent woman. Her father had somewhat reluctantly joined the Jacobite Rising of 1715, but later received a royal pardon and never again associated himself with the Jacobite cause. It was, however, a different matter for his daughter. At the age of 18, Anne married clan chief Aeneas Mackintosh, some 20 years her senior, and an officer in the Black Watch regiment.

Having tried unsuccessfully to persuade her husband to join the Jacobite cause, Lady Anne, undaunted, proceeded to raise a regiment for the Prince. Alexander du Boyer wrote of her:

Portrait of Lady Anne Mackintosh, attributed to Bartholomew Dandridge (1691–c1755). Her brooch, which bears a portrait of Prince Charles, was at one time overpainted with lace

> 'The intrepid lady, a pistol in one hand and money in the other, traversed the country; menaced, gave, promised and within fifteen days brought together 600 men. She sent half the men to Falkirk, where they arrived the night before the battle. She retained the other half to guard against her husband and Loudon, who at Inverness, were but three leagues from her house.'

On 16 February 1746 Lady Anne entertained Prince Charles at Moy Hall, her family home south of Inverness. News of the Prince's whereabouts reached Lord Loudon, one of the government's commanders, who planned to surround the house and capture the Prince. Fearing an attack, Charles left Moy Hall to take sanctuary in a nearby wood and, as Loudon's men approached, Lady Anne's blacksmith and a handful of men created the impression that the house was defended by a substantial force. Loudon retreated back to Inverness.

The Duke of Cumberland remarked in a letter: 'The General Villany and infidelity of the Highlanders open itself every day more, for whilst my Lord Seaforth and Mr Macintosh are with Lord Loudon, their wives are in open rebellion.'

When Aeneas Mackintosh was captured by Jacobites, Charles sent him back to the custody of his wife. Just before the battle of Culloden, Lady Anne's household accounts record purchases of 'white riband', presumably for making white cockades for the Jacobite troops. After Culloden, Lady Anne was taken prisoner but was well treated and was soon released. She died in 1784 and is buried in Leith.

The army recalled

In George II's government, the Duke of Newcastle, Secretary of State for the Southern Department – one of the two great offices of foreign affairs – was the first to take the Jacobite threat seriously. He had written twice to the Duke of Cumberland soon after the Prince had landed in Scotland, warning him of the need to return troops from Flanders. Cumberland's response was dismissive: believing the threat in Flanders to be greater, he was determined to retain his regiments and maintain his strength overseas. His stance was shared by others in the government, up to the King himself. But by 4 September, the situation was beginning to be taken more seriously and Cumberland was directed to send back ten regiments. The following day government orders were issued for the raising of county militias.

Any last doubters were finally persuaded of the Jacobite threat when news of Cope's defeat at the battle of Prestonpans reached London three weeks later. The dispatch on 24 September recorded: *'… this morning about day break Sir John Cope and his army were attackt by the Rebells, and Intirely defeat.'* The news was met with alarm. Cumberland and the remainder of the requested troops were ordered to return to England.

On 1 October 1745 George II ordered an 11,000-strong force of cavalry and infantry under the command of Field-Marshal Wade to march to Scotland. Facing atrocious weather and with inadequate food and clothing, the men were ill-equipped to tackle the Jacobite threat. Slowly and laboriously, Wade's troops made their way to Newcastle, where they took up position in this strategic town that supplied coal and fuel to London. To block any Jacobite attempt in the west, King George sent a further 10,700 men north to Chester, under the command of Sir John Ligonier. At Lichfield, Ligonier fell ill, and in November the king appointed his son, the Duke of Cumberland, to take charge of the army. It was a popular move. Despite Cumberland's previous command having ended in defeat at Fontenoy, his energy, decisiveness and courageousness marked him out to many of the British people as the one man who could put a stop to the career of the ambitious Charles Edward Stuart.

Standing in Salute, an engraving showing government soldiers c1745, by Francis Grose

'I think people begin now to be alarmed, I heartily wish they had been so a little sooner.'

Duke of Newcastle to Viscount Lonsdale, 5 September 1745.

Prince William Augustus, Duke of Cumberland

Known as:	HRH The Duke of Cumberland, HRH Prince William Augustus of Wales
Born:	15 April 1721, Leicester House, London
Died:	31 October 1765, London
Buried:	Westminster Abbey, London
Occupation:	British General
Father:	George II
Mother:	Caroline of Ansbach
Married:	Unmarried
Children:	No heirs
Image:	Miniature of the Duke by Christian Friedrich Zincke, 1743–5

Walter Grossett

Walter Grossett was descended from a French family. In 1728 he became a collector of customs at Alloa. He proved good at his job, seizing many large consignments of contraband from smugglers. He also served as a Justice of the Peace, and when the Jacobite campaign began in 1745, Grossett was given orders by the Lord Advocate to seize all vessels on the north side of the Forth to stop the Jacobites attacking. Grossett successfully carried out the orders, commenting:

'the Rebels after various attempts, finding themselves disappointed in their designs were obliged to march their army from Perth round the heads of the Forth and cross that river at a ford some miles above Stirling which gave time to the Kings Troops under Sir John Cope to return from Inverness to the relief of Edinburgh.'

When news arrived that the Jacobites had crossed the Forth, Grossett was responsible for removing all the boats, some of which carried arms and ammunition, from Queensferry and Borrowstounness (Bo'ness) to prevent them falling into Jacobite hands. He also played an important role in gathering intelligence for the government and acted as a go-between, urging the Provost of Edinburgh to defend the town. The Provost did not heed his advice, Edinburgh was taken by the Jacobites and Grossett narrowly evaded capture, losing his hat and wig in his haste to escape. The Jacobites plundered the customs warehouses in Leith, carrying off about £10,000-worth of seized and condemned goods. Grossett was charged with recovering these, but only managed to recoup goods to the value of £1,800.

As the Duke of Cumberland moved north with his troops, Grossett procured and dispatched supplies for them, including coal, biscuits – and men. After Culloden he continued to serve the government, collecting evidence against leading Jacobites and escorting witnesses to London. In 1747, the Duke of Cumberland recommended him for promotion to the office of Inspector General of Customs.

Hessian troop ships arriving at Leith on 8 February 1745, in support of the government; detail from a map of Scotland showing the events of 1745–6 by James Grante, Master of Ordnance in the Jacobite army
Map on loan to Culloden from the Drambuie Liqueur Company Ltd

Women of the Forty-Five

While women might not have been present on the battlefield, some played a vital role during the campaign. On the government side, which operated within regular institutions, there were inevitably fewer opportunities for women to participate. But some Jacobite women enjoyed a freedom of expression which allowed them to air their opinions with great frankness. They aided and motivated the Jacobite forces, sometimes helping to recruit men and provide resources, as well as carrying out individual acts of bravery.

Jenny Cameron led men to the Raising of the Standard at Glenfinnan, Isabel Haldane of Ardsheal encouraged her husband to lead out the Stuarts of Appin, while Anne Leith, together with a female friend, went out onto the battlefield of Culloden to help wounded and dying soldiers.

With friends in high places, few of the more famous Jacobite women really suffered during the campaign or its aftermath and none were prosecuted. The same could not be said of the ordinary women in the Highlands who had no such protection. Cumberland's soldiers, who regarded them as savages and as guilty as their men, committed horrendous atrocities against them. Accounts of killing, flogging, burning and raping make distressing reading. And some on the government side were appalled by the behaviour of their own troops.

Portrait of a Jacobite Lady by Cosmo Alexander, c1745 On loan to Culloden from the Drambuie Liqueur Company Ltd

Secret symbols of the Jacobites

Much of the Jacobite tradition was rooted in the Gaelic music, song and oral and written verse of popular folk culture. During the Forty-Five campaign, balladeers marched alongside the Jacobite troops, singing songs to rouse the soldiers. Pro-Stuart verses were set to familiar airs, allowing fiddlers or pipers to strike up a tune that Jacobite sympathisers would recognise, but against which it would be difficult for the authorities to act.

The Jacobites openly displayed their white cockade, a rosette or knot of ribbon, worn by the soldiers on their blue bonnets, which came to symbolise the Jacobite cause. Traditionally, it originated when Prince Charles Edward Stuart picked a wild rose and pinned it to his hat.

Many Jacobite symbols were far more subtle, often alluding to heroes from Greek and Roman mythology in order to depict Prince Charles and his father without explicitly naming them. The poet John Dryden's 1697 translation of the *Aeneid* is studded with Jacobite references, and the exiled King James

was frequently referred to as 'Aeneas'. The oak was also a symbol of the Stuart dynasty: when William of Orange came to power, medals struck in his honour showed a shattered and uprooted oak tree. In 1750 Jacobite propagandists responded by minting a medal with the text *'Revirescit'*, 'It flourishes again', depicting a fresh sapling growing at the root of a withered oak.

Jacobite drinking glasses were used to demonstrate allegiance to the 'king o'er the water'. Some depict portraits of Charles Edward Stuart, others are engraved with the Jacobite anthem and bear the cipher 'JR' for *Jacobus Rex* above the number '8', indicating James VIII of Scotland, Prince Charles's father. The rose motif occurs frequently, often accompanied by a stem bearing seven buds and leaves, in reference to James VII of Scotland. Glasses also bear oak leaves and the thistle as national emblem of Scotland. Other common motifs are a star (a new star was said to have appeared when Charles was born) and three ostrich feathers rising from a crown, representing Prince Charles as heir apparent, the Prince of Wales.

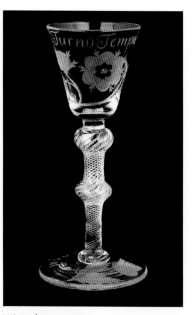

Wine glass, c1750, engraved with the Jacobite rose and buds, a star and a thistle. The Latin inscription, from Virgil's *Aeneid*, warns ruthless victors to beware their fate

'I could not venture to advise his Royal Highness to march far into England, without more encouragement from the country than we had hitherto got.'

Lord George Murray

The Derby Council and retreat north

Top of page:

The March to Finchley, painted by William Hogarth in 1749-50, depicts English guardsmen rousing themselves from a night of drunken revelry to defend London against an expected attack by the Jacobites

Two weeks after the Jacobite army had set out for England, they reached Carlisle and Prince Charles held another Council of War to decide his course of action. Four options were discussed: to return to Scotland; to march against Wade; to remain in Carlisle in the hope that English Jacobites would rise; or to march on towards London. The Prince favoured the last of these and his chiefs the first. And once again the Prince prevailed.

Showing astonishing speed, the Jacobite army reached Derby by 4 December. They were now only 125 miles – six days' march – from London. The capital was in uproar, the government panicking and the Bank of England in chaos. Neither Wade's nor Cumberland's armies were well placed to tackle the Prince's army. If London were to hold it would have to be defended by the government forces already there. While the king himself was preparing to lead troops into battle to defend his throne, there was increasing disquiet in the Jacobite camp. Lord George Murray and other Jacobite officers believed it was madness to attempt an invasion of London. They knew Cumberland's and Wade's armies were behind them and they believed that a third army defended London. Support from the English Jacobites was practically non-existent and the long-promised French help had failed to materialise.

At a series of crisis meetings on 5 December, the Prince's leadership was challenged. The Prince argued that they should proceed to London, while Murray and most of the Council insisted that they should withdraw to Scotland. Murray feared being hemmed in by the government armies on three sides. He argued that even if the Prince defeated one of these armies, the Jacobites could suffer more than 1,000 casualties, leaving them totally unfit to face another battle. The consequence of defeat so far from home would be certain capture and possible death. After much heated debate, the Prince's secretary, John Murray of Broughton, recorded: *'That the Pretender insisted to go on to London, but at last yielded to the opinion of the Council of War, and it was resolved to march back to Scotland.'*

The irony was that, in reality, Cumberland's troops were not quite as numerous nor as well placed as the Jacobites believed; and, as the Jacobites began their retreat northwards, the French were finally preparing to invade England. Unbeknown to him, Charles's gamble that his military success would prompt the French king to act looked as if it was about to pay off. But the Prince's problem was one of timing. His success had been rapid and he had gone into England before the French had time to mount their invasion. It could be argued that had he waited in Scotland, as advised by his Council, things may have turned out very differently. But as it was, the French got news of the retreat and cancelled their invasion, and support from English Jacobites never materialised effectively.

Jacobite and government forces

At Derby, the Jacobite army numbered around 5,000 men. To the north and south were government armies and militia which outnumbered them at least four-to-one. And yet until Culloden, the Jacobites went undefeated. To their advantage they were a light army; unencumbered by heavy artillery and baggage trains, they could travel quickly, covering far greater ground than their opposition. As they travelled through England they lived off the land, which provided them with rich pickings. By contrast, the government forces moved forwards slowly at a carefully controlled marching speed, accompanied by large supply trains carrying their food and ammunition.

The Jacobites gained a fearsome reputation for their devastating Highland charge, which could sweep away even seasoned battalions. They would fire their muskets at close range, then drop them and run at the enemy as one, roaring and shouting, to engage in ferocious hand-to-hand combat with their traditional broadswords. But the Highlanders ran into difficulty when they encountered modern fortresses such as Stirling Castle and Fort William. With no heavy artillery, the only attack they could mount was to lay siege to these impregnable targets. The government, as well as having the advantage of steady supplies of arms and ammunition, could also call on the Royal Navy to blockade many of the French ships attempting to reach the north of Scotland during the campaign. In the months after Culloden, naval patrols extended the threat of government power to even the remotest Scottish islands.

Life was tough for soldiers on both sides. Campaigning through the winter months brought great hardship for the armies. Appalling conditions led many to head for home. On the Jacobite side this was compounded by lack of funding and shortages of food and supplies.

Jacobite and (right) government soldiers depicted in the contemporary 'Penicuik Sketches'

Winning hearts and minds: *the propaganda wars*

The Duke of Cumberland and Prince Charles were distant cousins through James VI, who was great-great-grandfather to the Prince and great-great-great-grandfather to the Duke. When they met at Culloden both men were aged just 25.

The young Duke had no desire to be in Scotland, believing his true role to be fighting the enemy on the Continent, but he determined to remove the Jacobite threat once and for all. In February 1746 he ordered troops in the Highlands to 'burn and destroy' enemy lands and property. Orders stated: *'Such of the rebels as may be found in arms, you are to take prisoners & if any of them make resistance you are to attack them… And it is his Royal Highness orders that you give them no quarters'*. But in the Highlands many clans, such as Campbell, MacKay, Munro and Grant, were all supporters of the government. Archibald Campbell of Stonefield, Sheriff Depute of Argyll, recorded his concerns that innocent pro-government Highlanders would fall victim to a *'horrible scene of murder, blood and rapin'* by Cumberland's men.

After one such rampage in Morvern in the north-west of Scotland, Donald Cameron of Lochiel, one of Charles's loyal supporters, was so enraged that he wrote an intemperate manifesto blaming the Campbells for the atrocity and threatening violent revenge. Lochiel had been misinformed: very few Campbells had been involved. But the government seized the propaganda opportunity, publishing Lochiel's manifesto in the March 1746 edition of the *Scots Magazine* to demonstrate that the Jacobites were unruly rebels and savages.

Before long, prints and posters were distributed throughout the country carrying the message that a wild Highland mob, led by a Catholic dictator, had burst from the mountains hell-bent on robbery and rampage.

But propaganda was not restricted to the government side; the Jacobites used it too as a powerful weapon. As well as satirical cartoons published in the press, propaganda appeared in a variety of forms including engraved medals, miniatures and snuffboxes. Gaelic song was also a potent means of sowing the seeds of dissent amongst the Gaels. Gaelic was the first language of around a third of Scotland in the 1740s.

Spies were used on both sides too, another weapon in the arsenal of misinformation and intelligence-gathering. At a time when communication was slow, rumour and falsehood were manipulated by both sides and had a dramatic impact on their key decisions.

Top:
The Agreeable Contrast, a Jacobite propaganda print of 1746. Prince Charles and Jacobite heroine Flora MacDonald, surrounded by symbols of fertility, are contrasted with Cumberland, in a butcher's apron and accompanied by a 'town trollop'

Right:
The True Contrast, the government response, depicting Cumberland as 'the Royal British hero' and Charles as 'the fright'ned Italian bravo'

The Road to Culloden

*'I cant see nothing but ruin and destruction
to us all in case we should think of a retreat.
Wherever we go the Ennemy will follow,
and if we now appear afraid of them their
spirits will rise and those of our men will
sink very low.'*

Prince Charles Edward Stuart, in a letter of January 1746 to the clan chiefs who advocated
a retreat to the Highlands following the battle of Falkirk.

*'Nuair a thàinig solas an latha's a thuig iad gur
ann a' pilleadh a bha iad, cha mhòr nach deach iad
air bàinidh le farran agus mì-thlachd.'*

A battle scene from the 'Penicuik Sketches', depicting either Prestonpans (September 1745) or Falkirk (January 1746), both victories for the Jacobite troops

Background: a contemporary plan of the battle of Falkirk

'When daylight came, and they understood that they were retreating, they almost went mad with vexation and discontent.'

Rev Norman MacLeod's account of the Jacobite army turning at Derby, in *Caraid nan Gàidheal (Friend of the Gael),* published in 1810.

Build-up to the battle

Retreating from Derby on 6 December, the Jacobite army marched north, still a force to be reckoned with. There was a rearguard action to the north of Penrith and, on 19 December, the Jacobites arrived at Carlisle, where Charles received word of reinforcements and promises of French help. As the Jacobites continued their march to Scotland, they left a small garrison behind to defend Carlisle, which they regarded as a useful base for a return to England. But barely ten days later the Duke of Cumberland captured the Jacobites during a siege.

On 20 December most of the Prince's army finally crossed the border into Scotland, having successfully retreated out of a hostile country from between two enemy armies – in itself a major military achievement. By Christmas they had reached Glasgow where they forced the city to re-provision them with clothes and money to the tune of £5,000, before setting off on 3 January 1746 to attempt an ineffectual siege of Stirling Castle. With more Jacobite reinforcements joining them from the north-east, Charles's men now numbered between 8,000 and 9,000. Despite the Royal Navy blockade, money and weapons continued to trickle in from France to the ports around Aberdeen.

Miniature portrait of General Henry Hawley by Christian Friedrich Zincke (1685-1767)

Meanwhile the government troops were pursuing the Jacobites. They too had been busy raising forces in Scotland throughout the western Lowlands, Argyll and the northern Highlands. With the government still wary of a possible attack on London, the Duke of Cumberland had been recalled to the capital and in his place General Henry Hawley was appointed as commander-in-chief in Scotland. Hawley had a reputation as a vigorous and brutal commander. His mistake, however, was to seriously underestimate his enemy and on 17 January his army was defeated by the Jacobites at Falkirk. Around 350 government soldiers were killed, while some 300 were injured or captured. But the Jacobites failed to press home their advantage, letting Hawley retreat to Edinburgh. Two weeks later news reached them of Cumberland's imminent arrival in Edinburgh. Charles was eager to confront the Duke but was once again opposed by his chiefs. Their plan was to consolidate the Jacobite army, which had been depleted by sickness and men leaving to carry plunder home after the battle. The way to do this, they argued, was by retiring to the Highlands where they would secure the forts and renew their campaign in the spring.

The Prince was vociferous in his view that a retreat to the Highlands would play into the government's hands. But he also recognised that with his chiefs set on this course of action, there was little he could do, complaining: '... *but I take God to witness that it is with the greatest reluctance, and that I wash my hands of the fatal consequences wch I forsee but cannot help.*'

As preparations were made for the retreat into the Highlands, the Duke of Cumberland arrived in Edinburgh to take control of the government campaign.

During the early months of 1746, the government was hard at work drumming up troops. Volunteers were recruited in Glasgow, Paisley and Renfrew, and Independent Companies comprising as many as 2,000 men were raised throughout the northern Highlands, playing a crucial role in preventing further Jacobite recruitment in the Gaidhealtachd, the Gaelic-speaking areas of Scotland. The Duke of Cumberland moved north through Scotland, securing his position by stationing men at strategic points. He arrived in Aberdeen at the end of February 1746, shortly after Jacobite troops had left the town. He used the next six weeks to lay in supplies, drill his troops and, crucially, to develop new strategies for the battlefield in response to the ferocious Highland charge.

The Jacobites were now fighting on home ground. One army under Murray and Lord John Drummond made for Inverness via Aberdeen and another, commanded by the Prince, took the direct route to the Highlands. On 16 February, Charles arrived at Moy Hall, a few miles to the south of Inverness. There he was received by the militantly Jacobite Lady Mackintosh, whose husband fought for the government. That evening a surprise attempt to capture the Prince by government troops led by Lord Loudon was successfully repelled by Lady Mackintosh's servants. Charles was safe but he contracted pneumonia and during the following crucial weeks was confined to bed.

Contemporary drawings from the 'Penicuik Sketches'

Above:

Hessian officers of the government troops in Leith, February 1746

Below:

A hussar of the Jacobite cavalry

Three days later, Jacobite troops entered Inverness unopposed and took Fort George. This was followed by the capture of Fort Augustus, but an attempt to take the strategically important Fort William from the government forces was unsuccessful and by early April the Prince had recalled his men to Inverness. Meanwhile, to the south, the Jacobites were inflicting damage on government troops at Blair Castle, Perthshire; to the east at Keith in Banffshire; and, to the north, at Dornoch.

But ill-fate befell the Prince on 24 March, when government troops in the north of Scotland recaptured the Jacobite ship *Le Prince Charles* and its precious cargo of £15,000 sent from France. With money and supplies already dwindling, this was a disaster for the Jacobites. To make matters worse, John Murray of Broughton, who was responsible for the Jacobite army supplies, fell seriously ill. Without him, army provisioning effectively broke down. In their desperation, the Jacobites turned to a young engraver called Robert Strange.

Promises to pay:
Robert Strange and the printing press

The capture of the Jacobite ship *Le Prince Charles*, with its cargo of money, left Charles facing the prospect of being unable to feed or supply his army. In desperation, the Prince turned to a young soldier, Robert Strange, who was a member of Lord Elcho's Life Guards. Strange was a 25-year-old engraver who had previously been commissioned to engrave a portrait of Charles while in Edinburgh. Charles now persuaded him to produce counterfeit money to finance his cause. Within two weeks Strange had designed banknotes illustrated with a rose and a thistle. He recalled: *'We now talked of a circulation of larger sums, which would likewise be required. I gave it as my opinion, that I thought they could not do better than issue notes in imitation of the Bank of England, or the Royal Bank of Scotland, in the execution of which there was very little labour.'* Urged on by Prince Charles,

Strange worked diligently, but by the time he was ready to begin printing on a large scale, news arrived that the Duke of Cumberland had crossed the Spey. The following day Strange fought at Culloden and after the defeat remained in hiding in the Highlands before returning to Edinburgh.

Above:

Portrait of Robert Strange by Joseph Samuel Webster, 1750

Above left:

Strange's banknotes were never printed. These prints were made from his plates in 1928 to raise funds for the West Highland Museum

Culloden: *the battle*

'I do not like the ground. It was certainly not proper for Highlanders.'

Lord George Murray, 25 May 1746

'... The fatigue of the night's march, joined to empty stomachs and light purses, with the Duke's coming up sooner than probably they expected, gave us considerable advantage.'

Donald Campbell of Airds, on the government side, to Archibald Campbell of Stonefield, 22 April 1746.

The eve of battle

On 8 April, with winter finally over, Cumberland's 'redcoat' army began to march from Aberdeen towards the Prince's army at Inverness. For the Jacobites the outlook was now grim. Many Jacobite troops were still far from Inverness: they had little money or resources and were tired, cold and hungry. By contrast, the government army was in high spirits and by 14 April they were encamped at Nairn, where the Duke received a warm welcome.

Meanwhile Charles was at Culloden House, just outside Inverness. With just three days left before money and food totally ran out, he needed to act quickly. Aware of Cumberland's position, the Prince planned for imminent battle, despite many of his forces having still to arrive. On the following morning, 15 April, the Prince's army marched out and took up position on Drummossie Moor to await the arrival of Cumberland. Around noon, news arrived that Cumberland's men were still encamped at Nairn: there would be no battle that day. The army began to disperse.

Desperate times called for desperate measures. Prince Charles floated the idea of a surprise night attack on the Duke's camp, to be led by Lord George Murray. It was Cumberland's birthday, and his men had been issued with a ration of spirits to celebrate: the Jacobites believed that they would be sleeping soundly and therefore more vulnerable to attack. Nairn was some twelve miles away and the Jacobites would have to reach Cumberland's camp no later than two o'clock in the morning. It was just possible, but it would be a huge feat for an army that was hungry, weak and exhausted.

An hour before the Jacobites were due to set off, men began to drift away in search of food. Murray and his fellow officers were alarmed. But Charles insisted they went ahead with the plan. The speed of the march was critical to its success, but fatigue, darkness and terrible terrain conspired against the progress of the troops. By two o'clock they were still about four miles from the enemy. With the approaching dawn, they would lose all advantage. Against the Prince's wishes, Murray took the decision to turn back. Most of the troops returned exhausted to Culloden, others collapsed on the march itself and did not wake until after the events of the following day.

Top of page:

Lithograph, published by T Bakewell in London, May 1746, showing the Duke of Cumberland crossing the River Spey to engage the Jacobite troops at Culloden

Below:

One of the 'Penicuik Sketches' captures the dejection of many Highland soldiers before the decisive battle

Joseph Yorke

Joseph Yorke was born in 1724 and at the age of 16 entered the British Army as an Ensign in the Duke of Cumberland's regiment of guards. He rose quickly through the ranks and four years later, in May 1745, was created Lieutenant-Colonel in command of the 1st Regiment of Foot. At the time of Charles's landing in Scotland, Yorke was serving in Flanders. He arrived back in England with the Duke of Cumberland in October 1745. By December, Yorke's frustration at not encountering the Jacobites was evident:

'My patience, as well as that, I believe, of the whole nation, is put to the stretch when one reflects that so many of his Majesty's forces should be in the field, divided into two armies, headed the one by a Marshal and the other by Blood Royal, and should remain so long without coming within reach of these brood of villains.'

Yorke and his men eventually caught up with the Jacobites on their retreat north from Derby. After a brief spell in London, Yorke accompanied the Duke of Cumberland to Edinburgh on 30 January 1746, from where they set off in pursuit of the Jacobites. By 15 April Yorke was encamped at Nairn and the following day, early in the morning, marched his men towards Drummossie Moor. Yorke wrote that Cumberland acted with *'great skill and military genius'* by leaving the road and going across country to within one-and-a-half miles of the enemy.

To Yorke, Culloden was *'so glorious a ruin eye never saw before'*. In the immediate aftermath of the battle, Yorke remained in Inverness, hunting down Jacobites. Ten days after Culloden he recorded:

'Since the battle the Highlanders have been in the greatest panic imaginable, burning

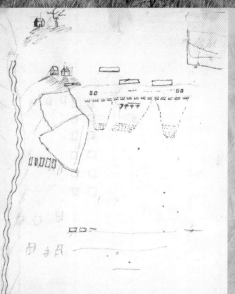

Above:
Sketch of the Culloden battlefield in Colonel Joseph Yorke's orderly book, done at the time or immediately after the event

Left:
Engraving of Yorke by Fielding & Walker, published in 1780

their colours, stamping on their white cockades, and cursing the Pretender and their chiefs who led them to that glorious field of slaughter, where freedom broke the chains of slavery.'

Yorke strongly endorsed the 'clear-up' after the battle, writing: *'We get great quantities of cattle and burn and destroy some of the country, but I hope we shall destroy much more.'*

Late in July 1746, Yorke left Fort Augustus for London. He returned to Flanders the following year and latterly served as British ambassador to the United Provinces. He died in 1792 at the age of 68.

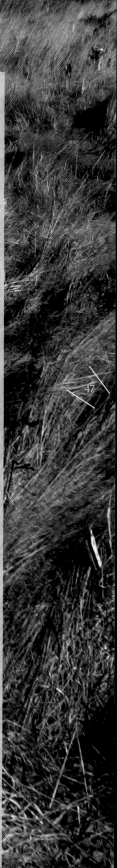

Drawn up for battle:
the initial position of the armies around 12 noon on 16 April 1746

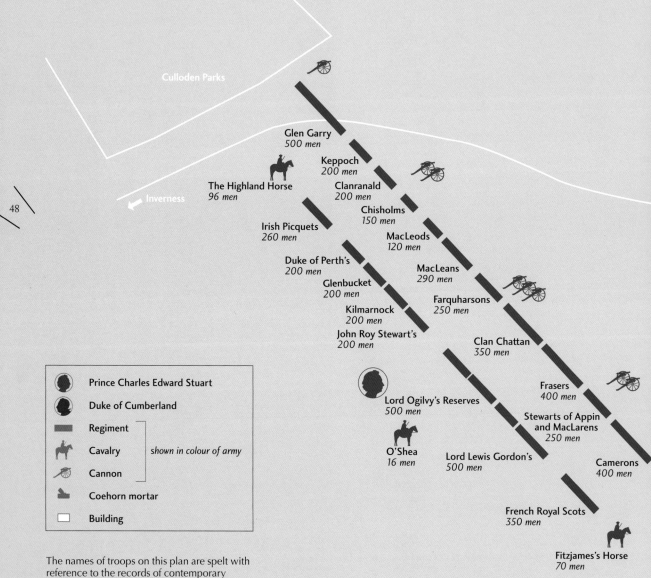

Culloden Parks

Glen Garry
500 men

Keppoch
200 men

The Highland Horse
96 men

Clanranald
200 men

← Inverness

Chisholms
150 men

Irish Picquets
260 men

MacLeods
120 men

Duke of Perth's
200 men

MacLeans
290 men

Glenbucket
200 men

Farquharsons
250 men

Kilmarnock
200 men

John Roy Stewart's
200 men

Clan Chattan
350 men

Frasers
400 men

Lord Ogilvy's Reserves
500 men

Stewarts of Appin
and MacLarens
250 men

O'Shea
16 men

Lord Lewis Gordon's
500 men

Camerons
400 men

French Royal Scots
350 men

Fitzjames's Horse
70 men

Prince Charles Edward Stuart

Duke of Cumberland

Regiment

Cavalry   *shown in colour of army*

Cannon

Coehorn mortar

Building

The names of troops on this plan are spelt with
reference to the records of contemporary
sources: Paul Sandby for the government and
John Finlayson for the Jacobites.

48

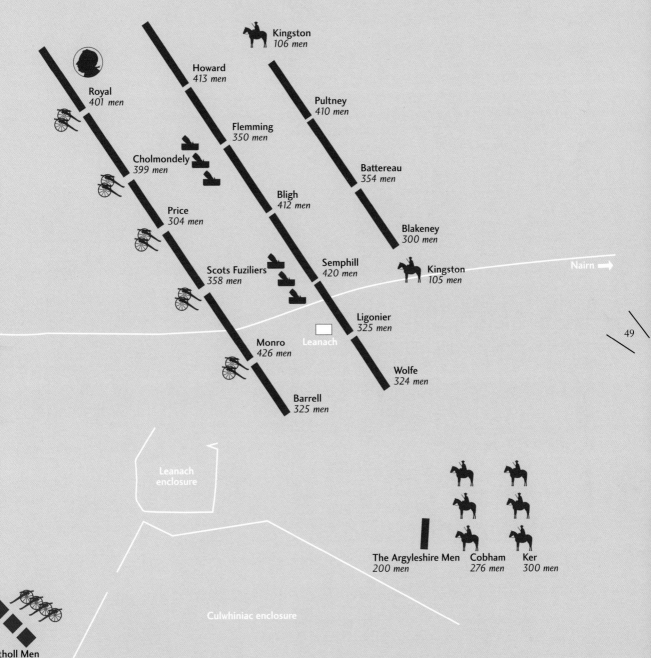

Kingston
106 men

Howard
413 men

Royal
401 men

Flemming
350 men

Pultney
410 men

Cholmondely
399 men

Battereau
354 men

Bligh
412 men

Price
304 men

Blakeney
300 men

Scots Fuziliers
358 men

Semphill
420 men

Kingston
105 men

Nairn

49

Ligonier
325 men

Monro
426 men

Leanach

Wolfe
324 men

Barrell
325 men

Leanach
enclosure

The Argyleshire Men
200 men

Cobham
276 men

Ker
300 men

Culwhiniac enclosure

Atholl Men
500 men

Plan of the battle of Culloden by John Finlayson, a mathematical instrument maker who served in the Jacobite artillery

The battle of Culloden

The contrast between the two armies could not have been starker. Just as the Jacobites were arriving back at Culloden around five o'clock on the morning of 16 April, exhausted and demoralised after their failed night march, Cumberland's men were preparing to set off to do battle. The government army had been encamped at Nairn where the men had toasted the Duke's health on 15 April, his twenty-fifth birthday. Rested and well fed, they awoke in good spirits on the morning of the battle to receive detailed battle orders.

Returning to Culloden in the early morning, many of the Jacobites went scavenging in search of food to fill their empty bellies. Living on only water and meagre rations of bread, they were weakened by hunger and exhausted from marching all night. The situation was desperate. Lord Murray later recalled: *'The last three days (which were so critical) our army was starved and this was a great cause of our night march proving abortive, when we possiblie might have surprised the enemy and defeat them at Nairn, but for want of provisions a third of our army was scater'd ...'.*

Lord George Murray was also in deep disagreement with Prince Charles about the decision to fight on Drummossie Moor, regarding it as *'not proper for Highlanders'*. The Prince had been advised by his adjutant general John O'Sullivan that the moor was unsuitable for Cumberland's horse and artillery. Murray, however, considered the ground *'for the most part ... a fair field and good for horse'*. Opposing O'Sullivan and the Prince, Murray believed the rough moorland terrain would be highly advantageous to the Duke but unfavourable for the tactic of the Highland charge, especially since the Jacobites would be coming under fire from Cumberland's powerful artillery.

An Incident in the Rebellion of 1745, French artist David Morier's depiction of the battle of Culloden, painted just after the event. He is said to have used Jacobite prisoners as models

Murray argued for crossing the River Nairn, where the ground *'was found to be hilly and bogie, so that the enemy's cannon and horse could be of no great use to them there'*, but his suggestion was rejected. The Prince was determined to fight on Drummossie Moor. Unlike Cumberland, who had been planning battle tactics for weeks and who had carefully briefed his men, the Prince held no Council of War on the morning of 16 April. In all probability he did not want to be dissuaded from fighting yet again, as Murray and many of his officers still considered a tactical retreat the wisest course of action.

Now as Cumberland approached with over 7,500 men, *'the Prince and the Duke of Perth, Lord George Murray and Lord John Drummond mounted their horses, ordered the drums to beat & the pipes to play, which Alarm Caused great hurray and confusion amongst people half dead with fatigue'* (according to an account left by David, Lord Elcho). The Prince ordered his men, who numbered around 5,500, to march out to Culloden and form up in battle order. With the odds stacked against them, many of the officers did not want to fight on that moor on that day, but they had no option: the Prince commanded it.

Jacobite weapons

The Jacobites fought using muskets as well as the traditional broadsword and targe, or shield, and they also had at their disposal dirks, knives and pistols. During the campaign several shipments of French and Spanish flintlock muskets reached Scotland. A number of government 'Land Pattern' weapons, the long guns favoured by the British Empire's land forces and known as 'Brown Bess', were also captured, notably at Prestonpans and Falkirk. After the battle of Culloden some 2,320 muskets were recovered from the battlefield; by contrast only 190 broadswords were captured.

Joseph Yorke, one of the government's commanders, was disparaging about the Jacobites' weapons:

'They leave in all places they pass thro' great numbers of their arms, as well broad swords and targets as fire arms, a mark that they are willing to return as little encumbered as they can, and that the arms, particularly their firelocks, were not worth the

carriage, and indeed I never saw such miserable implements in my life … collected out of the halls of ancient families but … quite useless at present.'

But if their weapons were not up to the mark, much of the Jacobites' military success could be attributed to their speed on the battlefield. They were lightly clad and armed, enabling them to carry out their devastating tactic of the Highland charge. *The Gentlemen's Magazine* of 1745 recounted that:

'The arms of the Highlanders are a musket, and a broadsword and target; the manner of fighting is to fire at about 30 yards distance, then fling down their muskets, and run in upon the enemy with their swords and targets, and I think their weapons have much advantage of our musket and bayonet, after we have discharged, as they take the point of the bayonet upon their target, and cut at the same time with their broadswords.'

This Highland targe is decorated with silver trophies and a central Medusa head. It was made in 1740, probably for James, Duke of Perth, as a gift to Prince Charles (Warwick Castle)

The Jacobites had perfected the technique of using their targes to catch their opponents' bayonets and flick them aside while at the same time wreaking havoc with their swords. But at the battle of Culloden, the Duke of Cumberland ordered his troops to thrust their bayonets at the Jacobites' exposed right flank, which prevented the bayonets being caught on the targes: a tactic which may have influenced the outcome of the battle.

'... Nothing could be more desperate than their attack, or more properly received. Those in the front were spitted with Bayonets; those in the Flank were tore to pieces by the musquetry and grape shot.'

Charles Whitefoord, government supporter, on the battle of Culloden, to Archibald Campbell of Stonefield, 22 April 1746.

The armies engage

Charles ordered the Jacobite guns to sound to bring his troops to form two lines. To the rear was his cavalry, numbering fewer than 200, and in the front his artillery of twelve cannon forming batteries, on the right, left and centre of the front line. Bitter arguments raged between the Prince's senior commanders over their positions, and key defensive areas on either side of the army remained dangerously unguarded. The army was missing those regiments which were still travelling from Inverness and was further depleted by soldiers who had failed to return from their search for food and rest.

By noon, in driving rain, Cumberland's army came into view, surprising the Jacobites, who were still forming their line in battle order. Their position was further back than it had been when they had taken up their posts the previous day in anticipation of battle and, instead of being surrounded by open field, they now had stone enclosure walls on their right and left. Murray believed that the walls afforded protection to his troops. He was, however, aware that he did not have enough men to occupy the enclosures, and that leaving them empty offered the enemy the possibility of infiltrating them and outflanking the Jacobites. In the event, this is precisely what happened.

The government troops marched confidently towards the enemy in well-disciplined columns and took up their battle positions, ending up in two lines. The Jacobites' bagpipes sounded. Cumberland advanced with drums beating and colours flying. The Prince's artillery opened fire first but had little impact. As the British army fired their cannon, tearing holes in the Jacobite ranks, Charles sent orders to Murray to advance, but Murray delayed. It may have been at this time that the government artillery switched from round shot to grapeshot, with devastating effect upon the Jacobites. In the face of such crushing assault, which was tantamount to a slow suicide, the Highlanders were eager to advance but were under strict orders to remain in position until the command was given. According to the Jacobite Lord Elcho, *'The Duke's army continued always advancing and keeping a continued fire both of Cannon and muskettery, which killed a vast amount of the prince's people.'*

Coloured lithograph by Luke Sullivan, after Augustin Heckel, 1747. It shows the Battle of Culloden with Cumberland in the foreground

Eventually when the men could take no more of the government lines' bombardment, the Jacobites charged, unleashing their fury. But despite their bravery, speed and ferocity, the advance was ultimately ineffective. Those on the left side were literally bogged down in the marshy ground. The lie of the land forced others to veer right, concentrating their attack on only a section of the government troops: this fatally diminished the impact of the charge, as well as obstructing the following regiments. The Highland charge was built on the tactic of running upon the enemy *'with the utmost speed so as only to receive one fire or at most two before they mixt'*. But at Culloden, wrote Lord George Murray in a letter a month after the battle, *'they were quite in disorder & received several fires before they could come up with the enemy who stood upon their first ground & the Highlanders lost the benefit of their own fire for only a few who ran the quickest actually fired upon the enemy, by far the greater number who followed as fast as they were able could not fire as some of their own men were betwixt them and the enemy.'* The attackers, not being parallel to their opponents, were all at different distances from the Hanoverian front.

Despite this, a large number of Jacobites reached the government lines. Facing their enemy, they also came under fire from those government troops who had penetrated the enclosure walls flanking them. Battling on, the right flank of the Jacobites with sword in hand broke through the first line of troops on the government's left and was only halted by Cumberland's second line of defence. The fighting became bitter hand-to-hand combat. Captain Clifton, on the government side, later recounted that: *'In the midst of this action the officer that led the Camerons, called to me to take quarter; which I refused, and bid the scoundrel advance. He did and fired at me but providentially missed his mark. I then shot him dead and took his pistol and dirk, which are extremely neat.'*

Outnumbered, outfought and outmanoeuvred, the Jacobites sustained heavy casualties. Those that had broken through were outflanked and trapped by the Duke's men, armed with deadly bayonets. Leading the right wing, Lord George Murray attempted to rally his troops by bringing up reinforcements from the second line but, in the onslaught of government fire, it proved ineffectual. The fighting was violent, terrifying and savage. Accounts tell of heads being *'cleft from crown to collarbone'*, of arms severed, of bodies rammed through and skewered by bayonets. Under brutal gunfire the Jacobites were forced to retreat before the left wing had engaged with their enemy. Lord Elcho recounted, *'The first line of the prince's army rushed forward to attack that of the Duke, and in this movement, as they had to face a terrible fire of guns and musketry, the entire left wing of the Prince's army wheeled round and fled.'*

With the Jacobites now in utter disarray, the Duke ordered in his dragoons. According to an officer on Cumberland's side, the heavily-armed mounted soldiers *'closed in upon them from both wings, and then followed a general carnage. The moor was covered with blood; and our men, what with killing the enemy, dabbling their feet in the blood, and splashing it about one another, looked like so many butchers.'* Another wrote: *'Our light horse and Dragoons were speedily sent after them, and strew'd the road for 5 miles with dead bodies.'*

In less than an hour the battle was over. A shocked Prince Charles watched from safety as the Duke of Cumberland emerged victorious. Around 1,250 Jacobites were dead, a similar number were wounded, and 376 prisoners taken. By contrast the government forces suffered only around 50 fatalities with less than 300 wounded.

'What, then can justify the deliberate folly and madness of fighting under such circumstances?

But our time was come. We were at variance within ourselves: Irish intriguers and French politics were too predominant in our councils. These gentlemen forsooth, considered themselves as to be but prisoners of war, whilst every other individual, were fighting with halters around their necks.'

Robert Strange, engraver and soldier in Lord Elcho's Life Guards

'It was here that the author of the forgoing part of this journal was killed and of 200 and upward of the McLeans there did not remain 100 men ... In this battell the greatest Barbaritys was committed that ever was heard to be done by Either Cristians turks or Pagans, I mean by our Enemies who gave no quarters Kild our men that was wounded in cold blood and continued so doing for three or four days or any others they could catch.'

Last entry written by Donald Maclean in the journal of John Maclean who was killed at some point during the battle of Culloden

'I shall only add that the Prince submitted with patience to his adverse fortune, was cheerful, and frequently desired those that were with him to be so. He was cautious when in the greatest danger, never at a loss in resolving what to, with uncommon fortitude. He regretted more the distress of those who had suffered for adhering to his interest than the hardships and dangers he was hourly exposed to. To conclude, he **possesses all the virtues that form the character of a HERO and GREAT PRINCE.'**

John Cameron, Clergyman in Lochiel's regiment

'There never was a more compleat victory obtain'd.

We got all the enemies cannon, ammunition and a great part of their baggage. His R.H. acted not only the part of a Generall, but aid de camp, was all the time in the lines giving orders with the same coolness as a judge sitting on his bench.'

Donald Campbell of Airds, Militiaman and Gael

You know the pursuit was very bloody, and are no stranger to the other circumstances that followed. The number of the enemy very much exceeded ours in the morning but was very much reduc'd before sun set, the killed and prisoners amounting to upwards of 3000 besides numbers that crauled off and died in the woods. I believe the Clans never had so good a brush before, and if ever they are clans again will remember it for some generations.'

Charles Whitefoord, Scottish Lieutenant-Colonel of 5th Marines

'I never saw such dreadful slaughter wee had made lying as thick as if they had grounded their arms and our men gave no quarter to them ... It was a glorious victory and I believe the cheapest that ever was gained our whole loss being under three hundred.'

George Stanhope, Lieutenant-General of 48th Regiment of Foot

The metal detector survey of the battlefield (far left) revealed fragments of weapons and ammunition, as well as personal possessions such as this pewter cross (left). The position of these found objects has provided valuable new information about the battle

Culloden may have been the last battle of the Jacobite Risings, but it was also the first battlefield in Scotland to be subject to archaeological investigation. The first phase of this long-term project took place in 2000 as part of the BBC television series *Two Men in a Trench* and has since continued under the auspices of the National Trust for Scotland as part of the Culloden Battlefield Memorial Project. The investigation, carried out initially by Glasgow University Archaeological Research Division (GUARD) and latterly by the university's Centre for Battlefield Archaeology, has included topographic, geophysical and metal detector surveys along with archaeological excavation.

Perhaps the most obviously rewarding element of this work has been the metal detector survey, which has revealed a rich assemblage of metal objects related to the battle, including musket balls, cannon shot, mortar shell fragments, pieces broken from muskets, buttons, buckles, a bayonet and personal possessions – such as a king's shilling and a pewter cross. But interesting as these objects are, it is only when they are considered in relation to where they were found (their archaeological context) that they really begin to tell us something meaningful about the battle. The debris left behind after the battle, be it in the form of a fired musket ball that fell to the ground after missing its target, or a coin dropped by a charging

Highlander, are pieces of evidence which can be subjected to a battery of forensic tests.

The archaeological project has provided some surprising insights into the battle. For instance, the distribution of the finds and the location of structures such as field walls, which appeared on contemporary maps of the battle, demonstrate that the battle took place over a wider expanse of ground than was originally appreciated when the battlefield was first displayed to the public by the National Trust for Scotland in 1984. The location of the brutal hand-to-hand fighting between the Jacobite right and centre and the government regiments of Barrell and Monro, took place much further to the south than was previously thought, in the area known as the Field of the English. For us today this is fortunate since, while further north the land has been successively planted with trees since the later nineteenth century, this location has been left relatively undisturbed since the battle and it is here that many articles dropped in the fight have been recovered.

The vicious contact in this area, where Jacobite broadswords met government bayonets, has left a pattern of dropped objects which can be read as clearly as a signature etched into the landscape. For instance, this is the only place on the battlefield where a large number of pistol balls was found, each of them having been fired at the close range at which these weapons were effective. There are pieces of broken musket either shot away by a musket ball fired at close range or smashed off by the stroke of a broadsword. Buckles and buttons have also been torn off in the struggle. It is here that musket balls were found in their greatest numbers, some of them indicating the lines of men who fired them into the seething mass of the enemy. To an extent we can tell which were fired by the Jacobites and which by the government troops, as the Jacobites used French muskets with a slightly smaller calibre than the Brown Bess. This is not to say that every Brown Bess bullet was fired by a redcoat – large numbers of these weapons had been captured by the Jacobites after earlier victories at the battles of Prestonpans and Falkirk. Even without considering this last factor, however, it is clear that the Jacobites were using their muskets more than has usually been considered: the traditional picture had them throwing away their muskets after firing one shot part way through the charge, some 50 to 60 metres from the enemy, and then going in with the sword. Some of the bullets found had been dropped without being fired, while some missed their targets, but others had been distorted through their contact with a human body and it is a sobering experience to handle and study one of these and think that they may well have killed another human being.

A new insight into how seriously the government army regarded the Jacobite charge has also been obtained through the metal detector survey. Very close to where the hand-to-hand fighting took place were found several heavy iron fragments from spherical mortar bombs which were fired into the oncoming Jacobites in an attempt to stop the charge. These were found so close to the front of the government line that there must

have been some risk of these unpredictable shells, which fragment when the powder inside the hollow balls ignites, killing men on both sides, or incurring 'friendly fire' as we call it today. When these fragments are considered alongside our knowledge of the hail of cannon fire and musketry into which the Jacobites charged, we must conclude that it is a wonder they managed to reach the government line at all. This achievement is certainly a testimony to the bravery of the Highlanders.

The mortar bombs did not stop the charge, but heavy musketry and tight discipline among the government ranks did. Despite the onslaught, the line held and a killer blow was delivered to the Jacobites when regiments in the second line moved round to deliver musket fire into their flank. When the fighting ended, more than one thousand Jacobites lay dead. Today the mass graves of these fallen Jacobites are clearly marked, but those of the fifty or so government soldiers killed in the fighting are not. One of the aims of the project was to locate these unmarked graves, and we believe that thanks to geophysics and a silver coin we are closer to doing that.

The coin dates to 1752 and is a silver thaler from the Duchy of Mecklenburg-Schwerin, which was one of the German Baltic states. It is possible that this unusual coin was dropped by a soldier who had served on the Continent but some time later was in the Highlands, perhaps stationed at nearby Fort George. While there he may have taken time out to visit the graves of fallen comrades when they were still marked in some way – perhaps by mounds like the Jacobite graves today. This coin may in effect be the 'X' that marks the spot, which according to the geophysics looks to be a large straight-edged burial pit sitting directly below where the coin was found.

Tony Pollard

The battle over:
no quarter given

The Duke of Cumberland's attitude to the Jacobites was ruthless. He wanted to eliminate them once and for all, capture the Prince and return to the main war in Flanders as soon as possible. Before the battle the Duke, determined to avenge the Jacobites' earlier victories, fired up his troops by informing them that Lord George Murray had ordered 'no quarter', or mercy, to be given to them on the field. The claim was untrue.

Within hours of the battle being over, Cumberland ordered his men to search out any surviving rebels in the 'neighbourhood of the field of the battle': they were to be exterminated. In accordance with contemporary practice, he viewed the Jacobites as traitors and rebels outside the conventions of international combat. However the French contingent, the *Royal Ecossais*, and the Irish Brigade were to be spared as prisoners-of-war. Certainly there were some on the government side who refused the invitation to kill, a few turned a blind eye, others preferred plunder to violence: but many committed dreadful atrocities, killing civilian men, women and children alongside wounded soldiers. Some of the most shocking incidents after the battle tell of the brutality of Scot on Scot, of Lowlander on Highlander and between rival clans.

Anonymous etching showing the Duke of Cumberland as a bovine figure holding butcher's implements. In the background, his troops set fire to an occupied Highland dwelling

The apparent order to 'give no quarter' was viewed by the Jacobites as a deliberate attempt to harden the government troops. The Jacobite supporter, James Maxwell of Kirkconnell believed, *'the impudent forgery of an order from the Prince to give no quarter could be calculated for no other purpose but to execute what was intended, and to divest the common soldiers of all sentiments of humanity and compassion, and to harden them for the execution of such bloody designs.'* It appears from existing copies that Lord George Murray's orders from 14 and 15 April did not contain an order to give no quarter, but a copy of the orders with the words inserted, *'and to give no quarters to the electors troops on any account whatsoever'*, does exist in Cumberland's papers. While Cumberland may not have been personally responsible for inserting the words, there can be no doubt that the Duke would have had the power, had he willed it, to ensure that few if any atrocities took place after the battle. Instead he embarked on a policy of 'pacification' which would have far-reaching consequences across the Highlands.

Above:

Government print entitled *Tandem Triumphans* depicting the defeat of the Jacobites, with Culloden House in the background. The title mocks Prince Charles, who used the motto (meaning 'triumphant at last') on his father's Standard at Glenfinnan

Right:

Travel pass, dated 21 June 1746, issued at Fort Augustus by the Duke of Cumberland. It allows the bearer, Lady Houston's waiting woman, to pass with some baggage from Greenock to Bordeaux

WILLIAM AUGUSTUS

Duke of *CUMBERLAND,* and Duke of *BRUNSWICK, LUNEN-BURG,* Captain-General of all His Majesty's Land-Forces in the Kingdom of *GREAT-BRITAIN,* &c. &c. &c.

Permit the Bearer hereof

freely to pass   from this Place to

upon   lawful Business, giving   all manner of Assistance   may stand in need of. Given at the Head-Quarters at   the   Day of 1746.

(By His Royal Highness' Command)

To all His Majesty's Officers, civil and military, whom it may concern.

Culloden: *the legacy*

'There is no European nation which, within the course of half a century or little more, has undergone so complete a change as this kingdom of Scotland.'

Sir Walter Scott, postscript to *Waverley*, published 1814

The aftermath

News reached London on 24 April of Cumberland's victory. The city went wild with delight, hailing him as the 'Conquering Hero'. In such an atmosphere, many urged the harshest measures possible against the rebels and rebel sympathisers. It was the clear intent of the government commanders to inflict such a crushing defeat on the Jacobite clans that they would remember it for generations. Cumberland let it be known that there was no mountain so barren or so remote that he could not personally root them out. Furthermore the Duke was content not to distinguish too carefully between Scots who supported the Jacobites and those who did not.

In the twelve months following the battle of Culloden, government troops launched a savage programme of repression to punish Jacobite Scotland and in particular the Gaidhealtachd in the heart of the Highlands. Whole communities around the garrisons at Inverness, Fort Augustus and Fort William were terrorised and hounded out. Women found sheltering wounded or starving prisoners were often strip-searched and raped. Those found with arms were automatically killed. Houses were plundered and burned, ploughs, farming equipment, boats and fishing tackle destroyed. Cumberland's army profited handsomely from the sale of the loot and plundered cattle, while those around them starved.

As adverse publicity began to emerge about the carnage after Culloden, copies of Lord George Murray's order to give 'no quarter' to the enemy went into circulation. Interestingly, the letter did not feature in the first official reports of the battle. In the months that followed the government kept up its propaganda, periodically issuing reports of barbarous acts committed by Jacobite clans as far back as 1716.

There are no reliable estimates of the numbers murdered in the aftermath of Culloden. The mutilated bodies of those executed were displayed as gruesome warnings. The message was clear: military uprisings against the king and government would not be tolerated. Many Jacobite captives who were not killed on the spot faced deportation and possible death: 3,471 were shipped to England and faced trial after prolonged imprisonment in Carlisle, York and London. Nine hundred and thirty-six of the Jacobite rank and file were sentenced to a life of slavery and faced deportation to the colonies in the American South and West Indies, 120 were executed and 1,287 were freed. Many others died in transit or in prison. Those Jacobite commanders who escaped execution on the whole fared better: some chiefs and leading clan gentry fled into exile on the Continent.

Above:

A contemporary engraving after George Budd showing the public beheading of the Jacobite Lords Kilmarnock and Balmerino on Tower Hill, London, in 1746

Below:

This list of over 240 people judged guilty of high treason for having taken part in the Jacobite Rising was issued by the government in September 1747. Noblemen come first, followed by professional men, tradesmen, then labourers

Ensign William Home

William Home was born in Duns in Berwickshire about 1731. At the age of 14, he joined the Jacobite army initially as Cornet and then as Ensign in Lord Balmerino's Life Guards. During the Jacobite campaign, he fought at the battles of Prestonpans, Falkirk and Culloden.

As Ensign, his duties involved carrying the Regimental Standard onto the battlefield. On occasion he acted as aide-de-camp to Prince Charles, who presented him with a miniature portrait of himself, a medallion and a quaich, a traditional Scottish drinking-cup.

Following the battle of Culloden, Home made his way to Ruthven to await the arrival of Lord George Murray, who *'made a short speech, which he concluded by telling us to shift for ourselves as there were no more occasion for our services'*. Soon after this Ensign Home was captured and imprisoned first at Stirling Castle before being transferred to Carlisle. At Carlisle he was tried and condemned to death – at the age of 15. His execution was set for 19 October 1746.

Whilst in prison under sentence of death, considerable efforts were made to secure a reprieve including a petition from Ensign Home to King George II.

'That as thereby your petitioner has justly forfeited his life by the laws of his country, his only hope is in your Majesty's Known

mercy and compassion ... When the rebellion broke out and your unhappy petitioner was first seduced to depart from his allegiance he was not fourteen years of age, one fitter to be employed at school, than in waging rebellion ... Your petitioner shall only add that if your sacred Majesty shall consider him to be a proper object of your Royal Compassion, the remainder of his life shall be devoted in praying for the prosperity of your Majestys person and government.'

Further petitions were made on Home's behalf by his family, who enlisted the help of the Earl of Home. In November 1746, Ensign Home secured a reprieve from the death sentence. He was eventually offered a pardon upon the condition of transportation for life. Ultimately he was exiled to live on the Continent where he became a Colonel in the Prussian Army of Frederick the Great. In 1774 he returned to Scotland where he lived out the rest of his life with his wife and five children. He died in 1794, aged 63.

Above, from left:

Ensign Home's silver gilt snuffbox engraved 'WH'; his quaich, or drinking vessel, engraved 'God bless King James 8'; and his flintlock officer's cavalry carbine (Logan Home Collection)

'You must never expect to see a total end to the rebellious spirit of this country till the Highlanders are unclanned, undressed, effectually disarmed and taught to speak English.'

Joseph Yorke, Lieutenant-Colonel of the government's 1st Regiment of Foot.

Prosecution and legislation

66

The government's fear of a future conflict with France on the Continent still lurked, so it was imperative that the Highlands were crushed once and for all. In the months following Culloden the brutal military occupation of the Highlands was designed to end any military and political threat to the government. Care was taken to destroy Catholic chapels and Episcopalian meeting houses, and areas, such as the West Highlands, where these religions were strongest suffered particular persecution. The government continued to maintain a military presence in Scotland, completing the mighty Fort George near Inverness in 1769, one of the strongest artillery fortifications in Europe.

But persecution on its own was not deemed sufficient to eliminate the identity of the Gaelic-speaking people of the Highlands. The government wanted to crush their very culture. In 1746 the government passed the Disarming Act, forbidding the carrying of weapons. The kilt and tartan, both potent symbols of Highland culture, were banned from everyday life, and were only allowed to be worn within the British army. Likewise bagpipes were outlawed as 'an instrument of war'. The Heritable Jurisdictions Act of 1747 deprived clan chiefs of their legal powers and Jacobite estates were forfeited to the Crown. For the many Highlanders who had fought for and supported the government throughout the Forty-Five, the implementation of this Act was a gross betrayal.

Some on the government side argued for leniency. Duncan Forbes, one of the country's leading advocates, supported the government and was known for both rigour and compassion. On one hand he believed: *'Arms in the hands of men accustomed to the use of them, brought up so hardily as the Highlanders, obedient to the Will of their chief … are dangerous to the Publick Peace and must therefore be taken from them.'* But on the other, he disapproved of the Act forbidding the wearing of Highland dress as it punished those clans who had remained loyal to the government.

Above:

This official pardon, bearing King George III's name, was issued to the Jacobite Andrew Hay when he was 67. He had fought at Culloden in his early thirties, then spent six years on the run and many more in exile abroad. He returned home only in 1763, at the age of 50

The Prince on the run:
what became of the war leaders?

Prince Charles had seen the slaughter of Culloden: some accounts tell of him being too shocked to move, others that he had to be held back from plunging down to rally his men. The day after the battle, around 1,500 Jacobites led by Lord George Murray made their way to Ruthven Barracks, only to receive orders from the Prince to disperse; now, it was every man for himself. In response Murray wrote a damning letter to the Prince accusing him of mismanagement, concluding *'had our feeld of Batle been the right choise and if we had got plenty of provisions, in all Human probability we would have done by the Enemy as they have unhappily done to us.'*

Three weeks later, on 8 May, the Jacobites regrouped again at Murlaggan, on the north shore of Loch Arkaig, in a futile attempt to resurrect their cause. But Charles had no fight left in him; he abandoned the remnants of his army and fled west to the Hebrides, where he spent a hazardous five months on the run. Charles chose his allies with great care and he was passed between loyal Jacobite supporters, never betrayed, but several times narrowly escaping capture. Famously, disguised as Betty Burke, maidservant to Flora MacDonald, he accompanied her 'over the sea to Skye'. Although this episode has become the stuff of legend, in reality Flora played only a minor part in his preservation. By all accounts the Prince's personality began to show a tough, moody, hard-drinking side, at odds with the romantic figure of folklore.

If the Prince was to survive, returning to France was his only hope. On 20 September 1746 he finally met up with a French rescue expedition on board *Le Prince de Conti,* and sailed for France. He would never set foot on Scottish soil again. Prince Charles was welcomed back as a hero by the French people. He was obsessed with the desire to win Louis XV's support so he could fight the Scottish campaign all over again, but in 1748 he was expelled from France under the Treaty of Aix-la-Chapelle. He spent the next decades undercover, drinking heavily and involved in futile conspiracies. Not long after his sixty-seventh birthday he suffered a stroke and on 31 January 1788 died in Rome.

The Duke of Cumberland was also hailed a hero by his own people after Culloden, but as news filtered through of his barbaric treatment of the Highlanders, his reputation was quickly tarnished and he was branded 'the butcher'. He went on to fight again in Europe, but his command ended in defeat and surrender. Culloden was the only battle he won during his lifetime. The Duke died in London on 31 October 1765, aged 44.

After Culloden:
life in the Highlands

The radical changes which the Highlands underwent could not all be placed at Culloden's door. Long before 1746, the clan system was changing as Scottish Gaels experienced major social and economic turmoil. Culloden only served to hasten the pace, as the Rising focused government attention on the region and its people. In the decades after Culloden, many Jacobites were drafted into the service of the British army – an ideal way, from the government's point of view, to integrate them with the rest of the kingdom. Against the odds, Highland military tradition survived Culloden and flourished in a new form under the sponsorship of the British state.

Some Highlanders saw benefits in the opportunities which they were now afforded to profit in the British Empire. Britain, having settled its civil war, could now focus attention on expanding the British Empire, which would grow in the following century to dominate the world. But for others, the destruction of traditional Gaelic ways of life presented them with an increasingly bleak and insecure future. Some Highland veterans ended up settling in North America, only to attract further Highland emigration. Twenty years after the battle of Culloden 'emigration mania' reached a peak, fuelled by the breakdown of old clan ties.

In the last years of the eighteenth century some attempt was made to redress the effects of some of the hostile policies imposed on the Highlands. In 1782, the Disarming Act of 1746 was repealed, and in 1784 many of the forfeited Jacobite estates were returned to their rightful owners. But increasing insecurity and spiralling rents impelled many surviving chiefs to break their traditional ties with their clansmen in order to make their estates pay, heralding the start of the infamous Highland Clearances. Life in the Highlands would never be the same again.

Top of page:
Watercolour by David Allan of a Highland soldier at Edinburgh Castle, *c*1785. Highland military tradition survived Culloden and eventually flourished again under the sponsorship of the British state

Right:
Engraving by Lumb Stocks of 1865, of a scene from Walter Scott's novel *Waverley*, in which the hero is introduced to Prince Charles. Scott considered Jacobitism 'a subject favourable for romance'

The Romantic Highlands

Twenty years after the battle of Culloden, James Macpherson published *The Works of Ossian,* his reworking of epic Gaelic poems in English. Translated into over twenty-five languages, the work became a literary sensation in Europe and encouraged the first tourists to the Highlands. Macpherson's work influenced the young Walter Scott, who would himself bring the Jacobite story to the fore when he published, in 1814, his acclaimed novel *Waverley* set during the 1745 Jacobite Rising. The interest in the Highlands and Gaelic culture was felt in the Lowlands too, as songs with a Jacobite theme flourished. 'Wha'll be King but Charlie' and 'Charlie is my darling' were reworked by Lady Nairne and Robert Burns to great acclaim.

Conserving the battlefield

The battlefield of Culloden, in common with battlefields all over Britain, has experienced considerable change since the day of the conflict that made it famous. The site, described by Rev Hugh Calder in 1793 as *'almost entirely waste moor ground with small spots of land indifferently cultivated, the appearance of [which] is rather bleak and disagreeable'*, gradually lost the appearance it had in April 1746. By the beginning of the nineteenth century, agricultural improvements had started to encroach on the southern part of the battlefield. And by the 1840s perhaps the most intrusive changes had occurred – the planting of a swathe of forestry and the construction of a public road through the middle of the site. During the last quarter of the nineteenth century, new farm fields and farmhouses sprang up and the conifer plantations were extended, leaving only a few small pockets of moorland at the northern and western extremities of the battlefield.

The land, and the adjacent Culloden House, was owned by Duncan Forbes, 5th Laird of Culloden, and one of the leading supporters of the Hanoverian government in Scotland. Duncan Forbes died in 1747, but Culloden House, although rebuilt in the 1770s, remained the family seat for another 150 years. By this time, the battlefield had become an important place of pilgrimage, not only for those with family or clan connections, but for many others who felt romantic nostalgia for the Jacobite cause.

In 1881, Duncan Forbes, the last laird to live at Culloden House, erected a memorial cairn and put up simple headstones to mark the clan graves. Public interest was also focused on the two old cottages nearby – King's Stables Cottage to the west and Leanach Cottage to the east. The Gaelic Society of Inverness raised funds to repair the thatched cottage roofs, enclosed the memorial cairn with railings to prevent vandalism and litter, and even suggested that the ever-widening road should be diverted away from the battlefield. In the 1930s, conservationists were driven to more radical action when a new building – 'Achnacarry', complete with tearoom and petrol pump – was set up at the very heart of this historic site. The National Trust for Scotland, which had been formed in 1931, took the lead in lobbying to protect the battlefield from further encroachment. In 1937 the late Mr Alexander Munro of Leanach Farm presented two small areas of the battlefield to the Trust. In 1959 his son, Mr Ian Munro, added to the gift, making possible the linking together of some of the Trust's properties. Earlier, in 1944, the late Mr Hector Forbes of Culloden had given into the Trust's care the Graves of the Clans, the Memorial Cairn and King's Stables, and sold for a nominal sum the field which contains the Cumberland Stone.

These photographs were taken around 1900 by James Hamilton Mitchell of Edinburgh, a visitor to the battlefield. The album containing them is on view at Culloden

From top: The stone marking the graves of the Clan Mackintosh; the memorial cairn; Leanach Cottage

However, the greater part of the battlefield remained in the hands of individual farmers and the Forestry Commission, and therefore still inaccessible to the public.

After World War II the graves area attracted a growing number of visitors. In the early 1960s the Trust created a car park about 300m east of the memorial cairn, and the Forestry Commission opened up two forestry rides and placed regimental markers to indicate the deployment of the two armies, based on research by Iain Cameron Taylor of the National Trust for Scotland. The Trust created an exhibition in Leanach Cottage and built a footpath linking the cottage, the car park and the graves area. But visitor numbers continued to mount, potentially compromising the conservation of the battlefield.

In response, the Trust, in partnership with others, began an ambitious conservation programme. A purpose-built Visitor Centre by the car park was opened in 1970 (and extended and improved in 1984); 'Achnacarry' was bought and then demolished; negotiations began with the Forestry Commission to acquire the afforested part of the battlefield; and the Highland Council was again lobbied to reroute the road away from the graves area. Eventually, a decade later, the road was moved and the forestry plantation immediately north and south of the old road was felled. Suddenly, the battlefield was transformed.

But threats to the site continued, primarily from the rapid expansion of Inverness since the mid-1970s, resulting in pressure to sell land for housing around the battlefield. The Highland Council designated the site a Conservation Area, with limited success. To prevent development, in 1989 the National Trust for Scotland, with the help of Ruth Berlin and Scottish Heritage USA (SHUSA), the Glencoe Foundation and CCS (now Scottish Natural Heritage), purchased the so-called 'Field of the English' and other land to the south of the battlefield – fortuitously, since archaeological research now indicates that some of this land formed part of the field of conflict. Funds permitting, the Trust may have to acquire more land to maintain the integrity of the area.